Cloud Migration for Industry: A Deep Dive in Best Techniques and Practices – Amazon Web Services (AWS) S3 and REST API examples and overview of Security Machine Learning concept.

Author: Sasibhushan-Rao Chanthati, Owings Mills, MD, 21117, USA.

Note: No Company or Organization is Affiliated to this Paper/Guide/e-Book/Paperback Book – work was completed on personal software platforms issued by Amazon Web Service for Personal development only.

Author/Owner - ISBN: 979-8-89298-462-1 - at Sasibhushan Rao Chanthati. email: sasichanthati@gmail.com (First Completed and published in the year 2023 and modifications made till dated 2024)

Contents

Introduction 3
Migration Tools 17
What Care Should You Take for A Successful Cloud Migration? 21
Product Design and development examples Sample Proof of concept of Minimum 24
Valuable 24
Financial data and algorithms migrated to the cloud include: 26
Detail analysis break down the algorithmic steps for cloud migration: 28
Use case for cloud migration in the financial industry with ML integration: 31
Machine Learning Model: A supervised learning model - Gradient Boosting Classifier or Random Forest to classify transactions as either legitimate or fraudulent. 33
Code Solution for a sample use case for the fraud detection using a random forest classifier: Python. 35
Use Case for Amazon Web Services - Simple Storage Service (S3) – Object Storage Service 37
Use Case: Managing the AWS S3 objects and bucket. 41
Use Case: Managing the AWS S3 objects and bucket using AWS CLI V2 – Windows 52
Useful Information for AWS CLI – S3 56
Use Case: REST Integration using AWS Glue ETL job (API as source end point and destination as AWS S3) 62
Benefits of Cloud Migration 72
Overview of Artificial Intelligence-Based Cloud Planning and Migration to Cut the Cost of Cloud 76
Advantages of Artificial Intelligence-based Cloud planning and Migration 88
Conclusion 92
References: 93

Introduction

Cloud is becoming a critical aspect of service delivery and digital transformation across industries. Organizations need an IT ecosystem that can deliver increased agility, innovation, and customization due to new demands from customers and shareholders, along with increased regulatory requirements. The process of executing a cloud migration is challenging and determining how best to structure a transformation to be achieved. I will discuss the challenges, methods, migration models, and benefits of cloud migration for the financial services industry in detail. Challenges of Cloud Migration. Change is not an easy thing. Changing the data infrastructure of an entire organization, in the any sectors, comes with its own set of challenges.

Apprehensions about security and compliance

It is common knowledge that moving IT services to the cloud brings immense benefits for the financial sector, but many financial services industry professionals remain cautious about making a move. With an increasingly hostile cybercrime environment, finance professionals – who handle enormous amounts of sensitive financial data – are often concerned that these data will not be secure when stored on the cloud. Simply put, finance professionals who must adhere to industry security standards seek assurance that the cloud technology will help them remain compliant and secure and alleviate their security concerns.

The excessive amount of technology debt and the lack of enforceable processes in the cloud.

Even though we live in a digital world, not everyone is comfortable with the excessive use of technology. Introducing a new technology for an organization involves setting up the database and software applications. Another major challenge is training the employees to use these applications daily as they lack skills at the initial stage. Inadequate training may result in costly errors for a sensitive area like financial services. Plus, the financial organizations have accumulated a lot of technical debt in terms of legacy applications, including home-grown and off-the-shelf products. The sheer size of technical debt makes the migration to cloud infrastructure a non-trivial task.

An unclear cloud strategy and non-committal executive sponsorship.

Any new change or a setup first needs a strategy and planning. The worst thing financial organizations can do is migrate the entire data into the cloud. With untrained and unskilled staff, there is a considerable risk of corruption of sensitive and critical data.

It is crucial to break down the process, know what to migrate first, train the employees, testing, trial runs, etc. Having a capable, skilled, and committed executive sponsor to manage the whole process is vital. Or else the entire process might end up in a disaster.

Total-cost-of-ownership can't be accurately estimated, forecasted, and managed.

Like all processes, cloud migration costs money. Even though cloud storage and computing are cost-effective in the long run, the initial investment is expensive. The challenge lies in estimating the cost of data migration and the training of employees, data management, maintenance, design, and customization of the architecture.

Types of Cloud Deployment Models

Every industry has its own set of requirements based on which a Cloud Deployment Model is chosen. Cloud Deployment is the process of setting up the virtual environment, type of access, size, security protocols, management, and other parameters. There are mainly four types:

1. Public Cloud

As the name suggests, the public cloud is easily accessible to the public. Data is stored on third-party servers, and the cloud service provider maintains the hardware. Thus, public cloud storage is inexpensive, reliable, and location independent. But this model has security and privacy issues along with limited customization.

2. Private Cloud

The name speaks for itself: Private cloud is accessible within an organization. It may be hosted internally or externally, but the organization itself controls the software and hardware. Thus, it ensures high security and privacy and is customized to the organization.

As the organization handles most of the architecture, it might be expensive.

3. Community Cloud

A community cloud is like the private model but is accessed by a group of organizations. Organizations belonging to the same community share the infrastructure while being hosted internally or externally. This approach helps in security, performance, privacy, and other common issues faced by the community. Hence this model is cost-effective and reliable. Many financial services clouds represent such a model.

4. Hybrid Deployment (Public-Private Clouds, Cloud-On-prem hybrid)

The hybrid model is a combination of two or more models. Both public and private clouds exist as separate entities but are part of the same architecture. The private cloud can store sensitive data and perform critical activities, while the public cloud can store fewer sensitive data and perform non-critical activities. Thus, it incorporates the best of both models.

Some of the financial services offered by these leading cloud service providers:

1. AWS for Financial Services[1]

AWS is short for Amazon Web Services, which provides platforms and APIs for individuals, companies, and government organizations. For financial institutions, AWS provides banking operations, secure payments, capital markets, and insurance services. AWS also offers grid computing, machine learning to automate payments, detect fraud, automate customer services, and many more.

2. Azure for Financial Services[2]

Azure is a cloud service created by Microsoft for building, deploying, and managing applications and services supporting many programming languages, tools, and frameworks. Microsoft Azure provides intelligent banking, modernized trading, and personalized insurance software systems for the financial industry. Predictive analysis using customer data, using machine learning to detect financial crimes and frauds, financial data storage, processing, and analysis, among other services, are provided.

[1] https://aws.amazon.com/financial-services/
[2] https://azure.microsoft.com/en-in/industries/financial/#use-cases

3. Google Cloud for Financial Services[3]

Another leading cloud service provider is Google with its Google Cloud, which runs on the same infrastructure that Google uses for its search engine and other products. Google provides Open Banking APIs, historical and real-time market datasets, analytics tools for trading, serverless data warehouse, document processing, AI agents for customer services and interactions, among others for the financial sector.

[3] https://cloud.google.com/solutions/financial-services

As already explained, Cloud Migration needs strategies. Here are the common approaches called the 6-R's of migration.

1. Rehost

Also called "lift and shift," this strategy involves moving applications to the cloud as it is without really implementing any cloud optimizations. Used for large-scale legacy migrations, organizations can save about 30% of the cost. Once migrated, changes can be done quickly.

2. Replatform

Sometimes called **"lift-tinker-and-shift,"** this strategy is a variation of the previous one. With this approach, only are optimized partially for the cloud keeping the core architecture the same. As a result, large-scale migrations not only save money but also achieve cloud benefits.

3. Refactor / Re-Architect

Refactoring is rebuilding the applications from scratch. Organizations that are looking to add new cloud-native features that were previously not possible use this strategy. This option happens to be the most expensive.

4. Repurchase

This strategy involves moving the applications from perpetual licenses to a new cloud-native like SaaS (Software-as-a-Service) platform. Getting familiar with the new platform and training employees might be the initial challenges, but customization, upgrades, and cost effectiveness are advantageous.

5. Retire

Retiring involves removing or turning off applications that are no longer needed. The resulting savings boost the business processes, reduce the number of applications, reduce cost, and allocate more resources to critical applications.

6. Retain

Organizations use this strategy when it is not possible to migrate critical applications. Such applications are retained and revisited in the future. Such applications may require significant refactoring or may not be suitable for cloud migration at that time. The above are the strategies used for cloud migration in general. The financial services companies have high-sensitive and critical data and thus need to decide a strategy first, employ experts with the right skill and knowledge, backup the data before migration, and maintain the system after migration. They need to ensure that data integrity is maintained, data loss is prevented, all the security and privacy issues are handled along with a smooth transition.

Migration Tools

Cloud migration is not something that happens in a matter of seconds. As mentioned before, it requires strategies, proper planning, and most importantly - tools. Here are some of them:

1. AWS Migration Services[4]

AWS Migration Services by Amazon provides many services like AWS migration hub, AWS application discovery service, AWS Snowball, etc. Some of their features are:

- Simple to use and a low-cost service as there is no need to install any drivers and applications.
- Minimal downtime as changes in source databases is synchronized during the migration process, thus keeping the source database fully operational.
- It supports both homogeneous and heterogeneous databases.
- It offers on-going replication even after the migration and keeps both the source and target databases in sync.
- AWS is very reliable, and the tool keeps monitoring the target databases and automatically restarts in case of any interruptions.

[4] https://aws.amazon.com/server-migration-service/

2. Azure Migration Tools[5]

Azure Migration Tools has many Azure migration services, Azure data migration assistants, and Azure Databox. Their features are:

- Automate Virtual Machines migration and data transfers.
- Supports migration across servers, databases, web apps, and even virtual desktops.
- Has a centralized migration repository that delivers end-to-end tracking and assessment of phases.
- Can make migration decisions based on built-in insights and recommendations.
  - Maintains data security and is cost-effective.

3. Google Migration Services / Migrate for Computer Engine[6]

Previously known as Velostrata, Migrate for Compute Engine is a migration tool by Google Cloud. The features of this tool are:

- Supports migration of both one application from on-premises and thousands of applications across multiple data centers and clouds.
- Has built-in testing for fast and easy validation before migration.
- The best feature is that it provides on-premise rollbacks in case of unexpected errors, thus reducing risks.

- Migrate for Compute Engine provides real-time streaming while ensuring data syncs and seamless transfers in the background.

[5] https://azure.microsoft.com/en-in/services/azure-migrate/
[6] https://cloud.google.com/solutions/migration-to-gcp-getting-started

- Automatic and seamless adaptations include driver/agent installations, networking, licensing, among others.

- Provides REST API for programmable operations and customization.

4. VMware[7] / Cloud Health Technologies[8]

VMware, a cloud computing company, acquired another cloud computing company called CloudHealth Technologies in 2018. Now hailed as CloudHealth Multicloud Platform, the acquisition expanded its cloud migration capabilities. Its features are:

- CloudHealth enables precision reporting, analysis, management, and more such business needs.
- Integrations with already in use communication, project management, and data analytic tools.
- Automate infrastructure actions like start, stop, resize and terminate. The customer's choice of frequency can schedule events.
- Provides APIs to initiate requests, view, create or modify data and write customized applications.

- Maintain security and compliance and notifies in case of security risks.
- You can customize graphical and tabular reports correlating datasets for analysis.

[7] https://www.vmware.com/in/cloud-solutions/hybrid-cloud/cloud-migration.html
[8] https://www.cloudhealthtech.com/

5. AppDynamics[9]

AppDynamics is one of the best cloud migration tools, especially when it comes to real-time monitoring applications. Here are its essential features:

- An end-to-end view of every application helps to plan, execute, and address technical and performance issues.
- Provides serverless monitoring for end-user to back-end application performance which you can view through a single unified platform.
- Provides AI root cause analysis and anomaly detection for monitoring. Thus, you can quickly address technical issues.
- Allows both pre-cloud and post-cloud migration analysis.
- Supports a range of platforms and technologies like .NET, AWS, Android, Angular JS, Apache, iOS, IBM, Oracle, SAP, and many more.
- Every component of the infrastructure - be it server, database, hybrid, and cloudnative environments - can be visualized.

The above are some of the widely used cloud migration tools. There are other such tools like Carbonite Migrate, Corent SurPaas, Turbonomic, Cloudscape - to name a few.

[9] https://www.appdynamics.com/solutions/cloud-migration

What Care Should You Take for A Successful Cloud Migration?

With the booming digital age, a financial services organization need to migrate their infrastructure to the cloud. But this challenging task involves a lot of security risks, and precautions must be taken.

1. Develop your strategy early.

Every business is unique. Each financial organization has its own set of requirements. It is imperative to develop strategies by performing a complete analysis of the current system, workloads, applications, and processes.

2. Determine which applications are suitable for the cloud

As explained before, not all applications need to be migrated to the cloud. Some applications might be cloud-ready, some critical but require a lot of customization before migration, and some might be just turned off.

3. Secure the right skills and resources.

Financial services are more about the services they offer. You must hire professionals with the right skills and expertise to ensure data migration and applications. Securing the correct migration tools and service providers is essential.

4. Maintain data integrity & implement a robust security mechanism

The financial industry contains sensitive, personal, and financial information. That's why you must take precautions to prevent any data loss—having a complete data backup before migration can mitigate such risks. Financial Risk Management is a critical area of concern for financial organizations. Ensuring that your cloud implementation is secured for vulnerabilities provides the stakeholders with the required confidence.

5. Adopt an end-to-end approach.

After cloud migration, the organization must manage its new system. The best solution is to be involved right from the developing strategies to their implementation. Such an approach helps manage the new system and controls cost, risks, and security.

Product Design and development examples Sample Proof of concept of Minimum

Valuable

Cloud migration for financial industries best practices to ensure data security, regulatory compliance, and efficient operations.

Key steps and considerations include:

1. **Data Security:**
Prioritize data protection and encryption to maintain the confidentiality and integrity of financial data during migration and storage.

2. **Compliance:**
Ensure compliance with industry-specific regulations (e.g., GDPR, CCPA) and financial industry standards (e.g., PCI DSS) while migrating sensitive data to the cloud.

3. **Risk Assessment:**
Conduct a thorough risk assessment to identify potential vulnerabilities and mitigate security risks during the migration process.

4. **Data Governance:**
Establish clear data governance policies and access controls to manage data effectively and prevent unauthorized access.

5. **Scalability:**
Cloud infrastructure that can scale with the financial institution's growth and handle fluctuations in data volume and processing requirements.

6. Performance and Latency:
Choose a cloud provider and architecture that can deliver high-performance and low-latency access to financial data and algorithms.

7. Disaster Recovery and Backup:
Implement robust disaster recovery and backup mechanisms to safeguard against data loss and ensure business continuity. Carefully evaluate cloud service providers, ensuring they meet the necessary security, compliance, and performance standards.

Financial data and algorithms migrated to the cloud include:

1. Transaction Data:

Banking, trading, and payment transaction data can be migrated to the cloud for secure storage and real-time processing.

2. Risk Management Algorithms:

Financial institutions often migrate algorithms for risk assessment, credit scoring, and fraud detection to the cloud to enhance accuracy and efficiency.

3. Portfolio Optimization:

Investment firms may leverage cloud-based algorithms to optimize portfolio allocation and risk management strategies.

4. Market Data Analysis:

Cloud migration enables financial institutions to analyze vast amounts of market data efficiently and make informed investment decisions.

5. Customer Insights:

Banks and insurance companies can use cloud-based algorithms to analyze customer behavior, preferences, and demographics for personalized services.

6. Compliance and Regulatory Reporting:

Cloud-based solutions can automate compliance checks and reporting processes, reducing manual efforts, and ensuring adherence to regulations.

Detail analysis break down the algorithmic steps for cloud migration:

1. Assessment and Planning:

Identify the financial data and algorithms to be migrated to the cloud. Analyse the current infrastructure and applications to determine cloud suitability. Evaluate regulatory and compliance requirements related to data migration. Define the scope, objectives, and expected outcomes of the cloud migration.

2. Data Classification and Security Measures:
Categorize financial data based on sensitivity and regulatory requirements. Implement encryption and access controls to protect sensitive data during migration and storage.

3. Vendor Selection:
Research and evaluate various cloud service providers based on security, compliance, performance, and scalability. Choose a cloud vendor that aligns with the financial institution's needs and regulatory standards.

4. Architecture Design:
Develop a cloud architecture that ensures high availability, fault tolerance, and scalability. Plan for disaster recovery and backup mechanisms to maintain data integrity.

5. Data Preparation and Pre-Migration Checks:
Clean and prepare the data to ensure accuracy and consistency before migration. Conduct pre-migration tests to identify potential issues and resolve them proactively.

6. Data Migration:

Transfer financial data and algorithms to the cloud using secure channels.
Monitor the migration process for any anomalies and ensure data integrity.

7. Application Migration:
Move financial algorithms and applications to the cloud infrastructure.
Configure the cloud environment to support the algorithms' requirements.

8. Testing and Validation:
Perform thorough testing of migrated applications and algorithms to verify functionality. Validate data integrity and consistency between the on-premises and cloud systems.

9. Security and Access Controls:
Set up access controls, authentication, and authorization mechanisms to protect cloud based financial systems.

10. Performance Optimization:
Optimize the performance of algorithms and applications in the cloud environment. Finetune resource allocation to achieve optimal processing speeds.

11. Monitoring and Maintenance:
Implement continuous monitoring and logging for security and performance analysis.   - Regularly update and patch software to maintain system integrity.

12. User Training and Documentation:
Provide training to employees on using cloud-based financial systems securely. Document the migration process, configurations, and security measures for future reference.

13. Compliance and Regulatory Adherence:
Ensure ongoing compliance with industry-specific regulations and standards. Regularly audit the cloud infrastructure to meet compliance requirements.

14. Disaster Recovery and Business Continuity:
Continuously review and update disaster recovery plans to ensure data protection and business continuity.

15. Review and Optimization:
Periodically review cloud performance, costs, and security measures. Optimize the cloud environment based on changing business needs and technological advancements.

Use case for cloud migration in the financial industry with ML integration:

1. Supervised Learning: where the algorithm learns from labelled data to make predictions or classifications.

2. Unsupervised Learning: where the algorithm identifies patterns and structures in unlabelled data without explicit guidance.

3. Feature Engineering: The process of selecting, transforming, and creating meaningful features from raw data to improve ML model performance.

4. Model Training: The process of feeding data to the ML algorithm to learn patterns and relationships between features and labels.

5. Model Evaluation: Assessing the ML model's performance using metrics such as accuracy, precision, recall, and F1-score.

Fraud Detection in Cloud-based Financial Transactions:

Objective: To detect fraudulent transactions in real-time for a financial institution migrating its operations to the cloud.

Data: Transaction data containing information like transaction amount, timestamp, account details, and transaction type.

Machine Learning Model: A supervised learning model - Gradient Boosting Classifier or Random Forest to classify transactions as either legitimate or fraudulent.

1. Data Collection and Pre-processing:
Collect transaction data from various sources and combine it in the cloud data storage. Preprocess the data by handling missing values, normalizing numerical features, and encoding categorical variables.

2. Feature Engineering:
Extract relevant features from the transaction data, such as transaction frequency, account history, and average transaction amount.

3. Model Training and Validation:
Split the data into training and validation sets. Use historical transaction data with labels (fraudulent or legitimate) to train the supervised learning model. Evaluate the model's performance on the validation set using metrics like precision, recall, and accuracy.

4. Real-time Scoring and Deployment:
Set up a cloud-based API to receive incoming transaction data in real-time.
Apply the trained model to classify transactions as they occur, providing instantaneous results.

5. Monitoring and Model Updates:
Continuously monitor the model's performance in real-time production.

If necessary, update the model periodically to adapt to new fraud patterns.

6. Anomaly Detection:

Use unsupervised learning techniques to identify anomalies in transaction patterns, which might indicate potential fraud.

7. User Alerts and Actions:
For flagged transactions, generate alerts for immediate review and potential blocking or verification.

8. Benefits:

Real-time fraud detection: With ML integrated into the cloud-based financial system, the institution can quickly identify and respond to potentially fraudulent activities, minimizing financial losses.

9. Scalability:

The cloud infrastructure enables the system to handle large volumes of real time transactions and data for efficient fraud detection.

10. Accuracy Improvement:

ML models can continuously learn from new data, leading to improved fraud detection accuracy over time.

Code Solution for a sample use case for the fraud detection using a random forest classifier: Python.

```python
# Required Libraries import
pandas as pd from
sklearn.model_selection import
train_test_split from
sklearn.ensemble import
RandomForestClassifier
from sklearn.metrics import accuracy_score, precision_score, recall_score, f1_score

# Step 1: Data Collection and Pre-processing (Assuming you have the data in a CSV file) filename I have given 'transaction_data.csv' data = pd.read_csv('transaction_data.csv')

# Step 2: Feature Engineering
# For simplicity, let's assume we have already performed feature engineering and selected relevant features.

# Step 3: Model Training and Validation
# Separate features (X) and labels (y) X = data.drop('is_fraudulent', axis=1) y = data['is_fraudulent']
 # Split data into training and validation sets
X_train, X_val, y_train, y_val = train_test_split(X, y, test_size=0.2, random_state=42)
```

```python
# Initialize and train the Random Forest classifier
rf_classifier = RandomForestClassifier(random_state=42)
rf_classifier.fit(X_train, y_train)

# Step 4: Real-time Scoring and Deployment (Not shown in this code example as it requires real-time API setup)

# Step 5: Monitoring and Model Updates (Not shown in this code example as it requires continuous monitoring and updating)

# Step 6: Model Evaluation
y_pred = rf_classifier.predict(X_val)

# Evaluate the model's performance
accuracy = accuracy_score(y_val, y_pred)
precision = precision_score(y_val, y_pred)
recall = recall_score(y_val, y_pred)
f1 = f1_score(y_val, y_pred)
print(f"Model Evaluation:")
print(f"Accuracy: {accuracy:.4f}")
print(f"Precision: {precision:.4f}")
print(f"Recall: {recall:.4f}")
print(f"F1 Score: {f1:.4f}")
```

Use Case for Amazon Web Services - Simple Storage Service (S3) – Object Storage Service

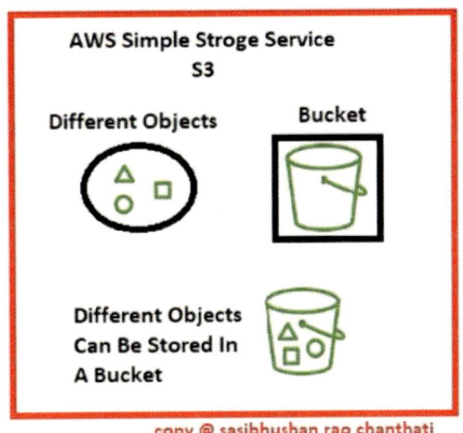

The data is stored in the form of files and block storage, managing data as blocks within sectors and tracks. S3 console – which will be an interface to upload and access to the data.

S3 Objects – The object can be files, each object will have key, value, version ID and metadata. The key is a unique name to the object. By default, the value is the sequence of bytes, every time version of the objects will be updated, and additional information attached to the objects is the metadata.

Buckets – The objects are stored in buckets and buckets can also have folders. Name of the bucket will be unique.

S3 Objects are like files which contains data, they consist of Key (Name of the object), Value (Data itself made up of the sequence of bytes), Version ID (Inserted and Updated Version of the object), Metadata (Additional Information attached to the object).

S3 Buckets will have unique naming, the S3 buckets will have folders to store objects.

S3 – Storage classes:

S3 - Standard storage class, which is available in different zones. S3 – Intelligence Tiering, without impacting the performance the ML will be analyzing the object usage and will be determining the exact storage class. S3 – Standard Infrequently accessed IA, One Zone IA, which is available only for one zone, Glacier – data retrieval will be very faster, this is for long term cold storage.

S3 – Security:

Whenever we create a new bucket, it will be blocked for public use, they remain private by default. The logging per user can be turned-on for a bucket and the log files are generated and saved in a different bucket. We can write complex bucket policy conditions for access, or we can give access to the buckets by access control lists.

S3 – Encryption:

Encryption in transit, traffic between the local host and S3 is archived via SSL/TSL. Server Side Encryption with amazon S3 managed keys (SSE – S3) – Encryption at Rest. SSE – AES S3 handles the key uses AES 256 algorithm. SSE – KMS Envelope encryption Its AWS KMS where user will manage the keys. SSE – C Customer provided key, client-side encryption – Users manages the encryption.

S3 - Data Consistency:

User put data or write data to S3, when user write new object, then the data consistency pays a main role. The data consistency will be different when we write new objects than deleting an object or over writing an object.

New Object (PUTS) → The consistency will be ready immediately after writing (READ after Write Consistency)

Overwrite (PUTS) / Delete Objects (DELETES) → S3 will take time to replicate the versions if overwrite or delete is done.

S3 - Cross-Region Replication:

Users can enable cross region replications to manage disaster recovery for the objects. When cross region replication is enabled, the objects will be automatically replicated to other regions when they are uploaded.

S3 - Versioning:

Once the versioning is enabled this can't be disabled, we can suspend it later if not required. The version ID will be populated. Fully integrated with S3 life cycle rules. When user deletes the object, this feature will provide protection.

S3 - Life Cycle Management:

S3 Life cycle management is an automated process of moving objects to the different storage classes (Glacier) or deleting them together. This process works with versioning, and we can apply rules for current and previous versions.

S3 - Transfer Acceleration:

Long distance users can access files from S3 very fast and securely with transfer acceleration. Users will be using distinct URL for an edge location instead of uploading to the bucket. When data arrives at the edge location it is automatically loaded to S3 over a specially optimized network path (AWS Backbone Network).

S3 - pre-signed URLs:

These are mainly used for web applications. These URLs are used for uploading and downloading data from objects. The URLs will expire soon based on the expiration time we provide. Users can create pre-signed URLs Command Line Interface CLI or by using Software Development kit SDK. The URL have Access Key ID, Expiration and Signature.

https://sasibucket.s3.console.aws.amazonaws.com/sasi1object?AWSAccessKeyId=xxxxxxxxxxxxxx&Expires=xxxxxxxxxxxxxxx&Signature=xxxxxxxxxxxxx

S3 - MFA Delete:

Multi-Factor Authentication (MFA) delete feature for S3 objects can be enabled only when versioning is enabled. To delete the object, the MFA code is required. Usually bucket owner can delete the objects.

Use Case: Managing the AWS S3 objects and bucket.

Overview:

In this use case, we will be loading/deleting images, documents (word, PDF, excel), videos to S3 buckets by creating objects. To manage the S3 objects in the buckets, first step is to create the bucket in AWS S3. The bucket created can also be deleted. Once the bucket is created the files can be uploaded into the bucket. The folder needs to be created in the bucket to upload the files. By default, the S3 buckets are private, but we can also make the bucket available for others (public access). Enabling versioning to the S3 Buckets. Encryption turning on for the buckets. Uploading and downloading files by using CLI. Pre-signing URLs for the buckets. Life cycle rules for objects. Enabling cross region replications for buckets and creating the rules. Custom rules for bucket policy for access to the bucket.

Steps:

Manual way to create a bucket – the bucket name should be unique. By default, the bucket will be a private bucket. But we can make it as a public bucket.

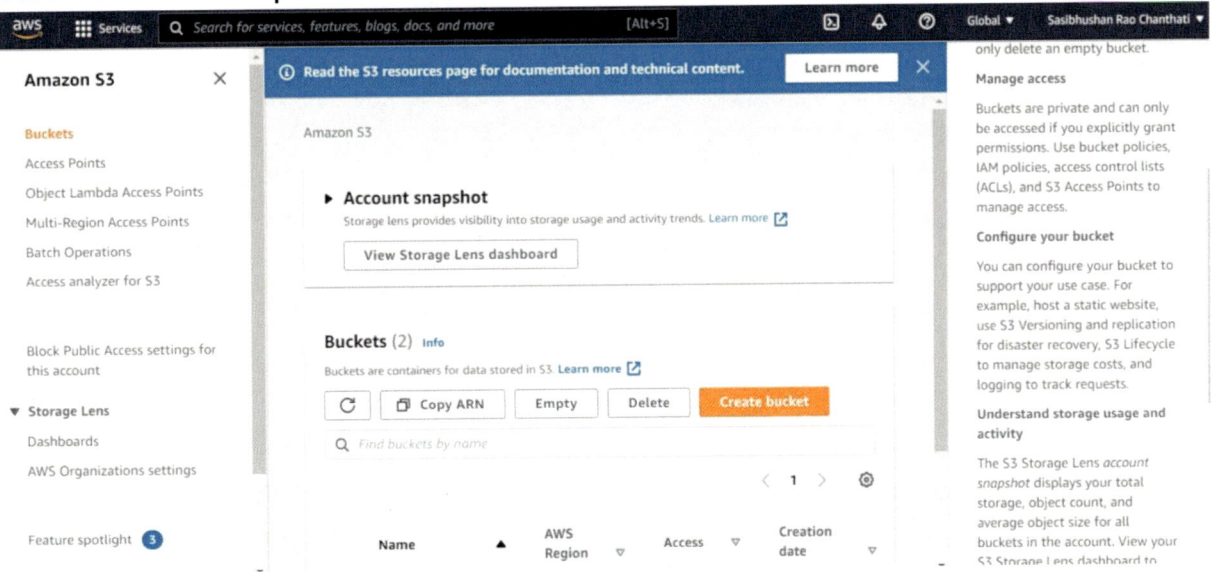

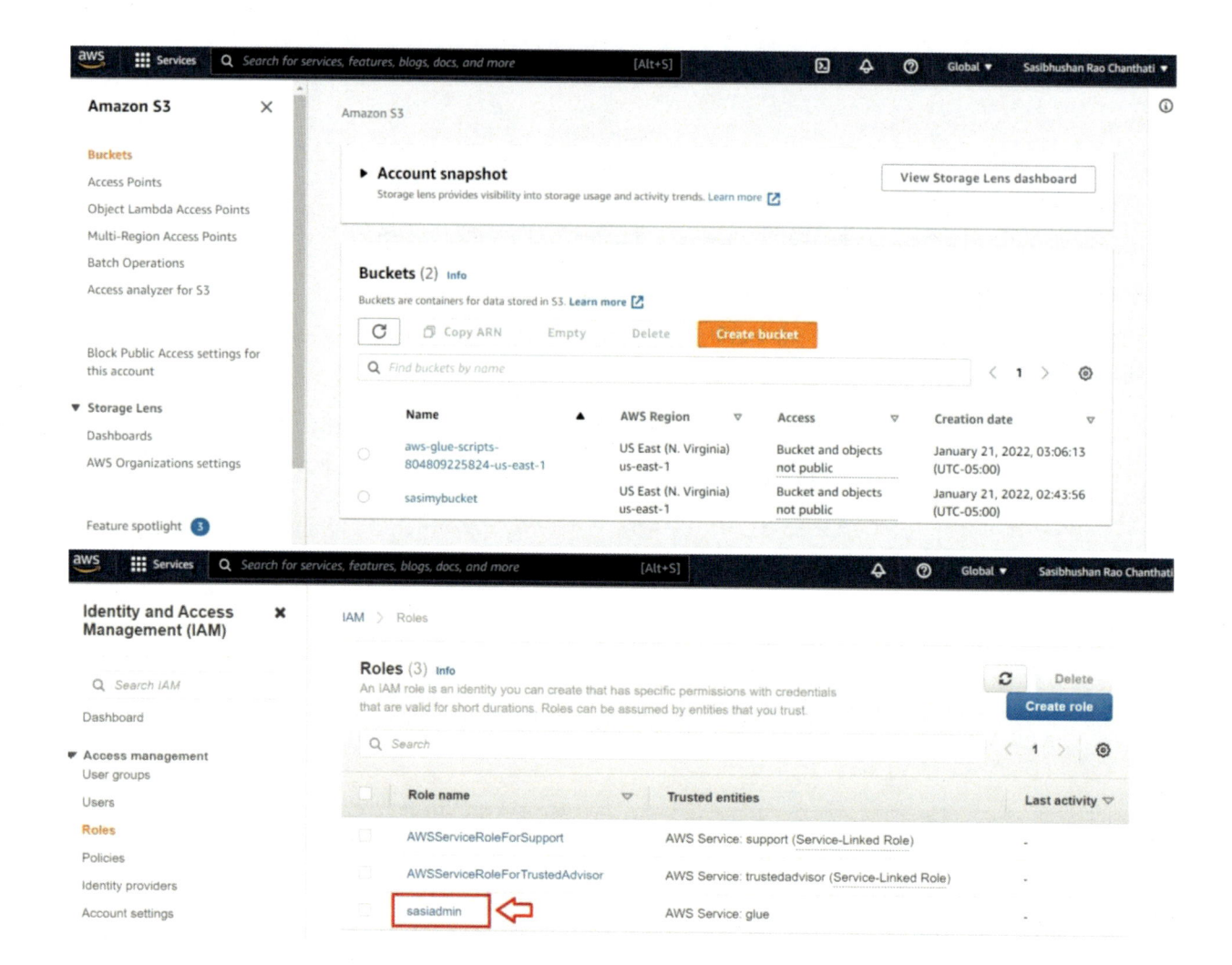

S3 Bucket can be created or use the existing S3 bucket.

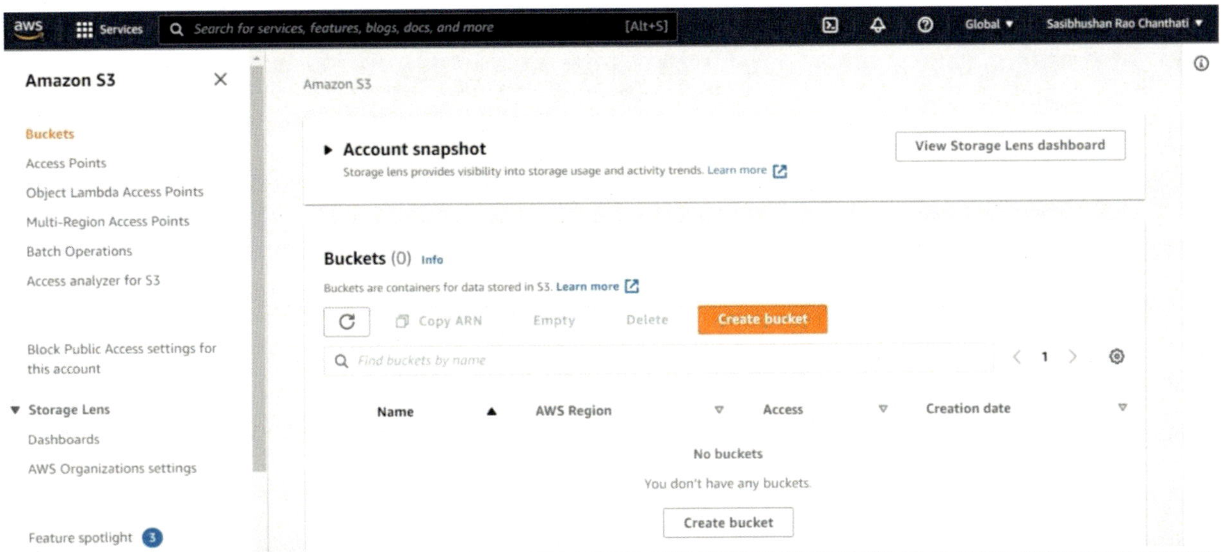
aws
Services
Search for services, features, blogs, docs, and more
[Alt+S]
Global
Sasibhushan Rao Chanthati
Amazon S3
Buckets
Access Points
Object Lambda Access Points
Multi-Region Access Points
Batch Operations
Access analyzer for S3
Block Public Access settings for this account
Storage Lens
Dashboards
AWS Organizations settings
Feature spotlight 3
Amazon S3
Account snapshot
Storage lens provides visibility into storage usage and activity trends. Learn more
View Storage Lens dashboard
Buckets (0) Info
Buckets are containers for data stored in S3. Learn more
Copy ARN
Empty
Delete
Create bucket
Find buckets by name
1
Name
AWS Region
Access
Creation date
No buckets
You don't have any buckets.
Create bucket
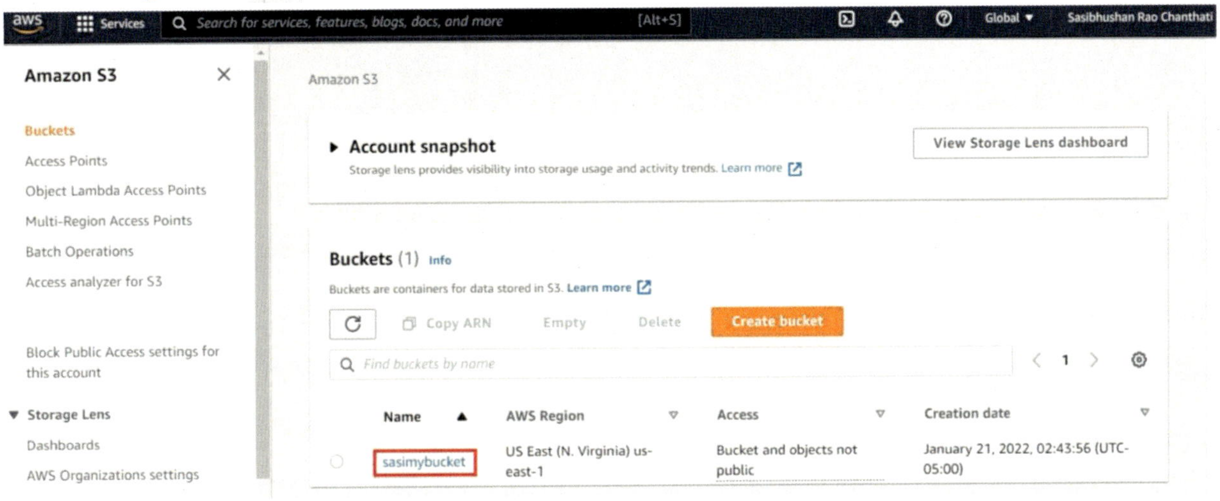
aws
Services
Search for services, features, blogs, docs, and more
[Alt+S]
Global
Sasibhushan Rao Chanthati
Amazon S3
Buckets
Access Points
Object Lambda Access Points
Multi-Region Access Points
Batch Operations
Access analyzer for S3
Block Public Access settings for this account
Storage Lens
Dashboards
AWS Organizations settings
Amazon S3
Account snapshot
Storage lens provides visibility into storage usage and activity trends. Learn more
View Storage Lens dashboard
Buckets (1) Info
Buckets are containers for data stored in S3. Learn more
Copy ARN
Empty
Delete
Create bucket
Find buckets by name
1
Name
AWS Region
Access
Creation date
sasimybucket
US East (N. Virginia) us-east-1
Bucket and objects not public
January 21, 2022, 02:43:56 (UTC-05:00)

Creating objects in the buckets is to create folders in the bucket.

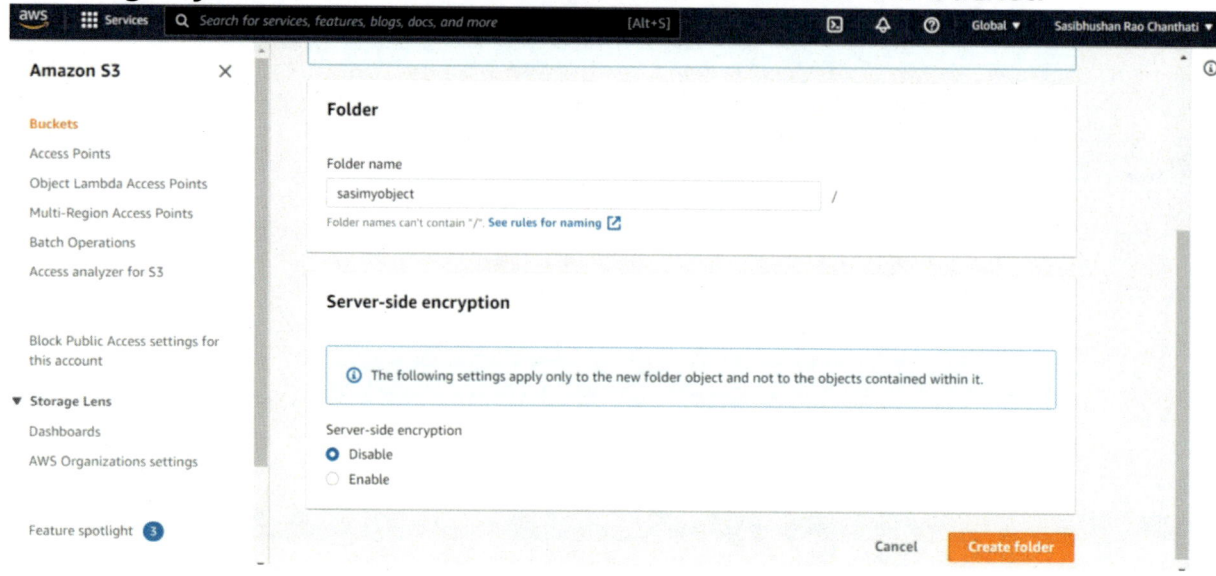

Documents can be uploaded into the buckets. Click on Upload documents.

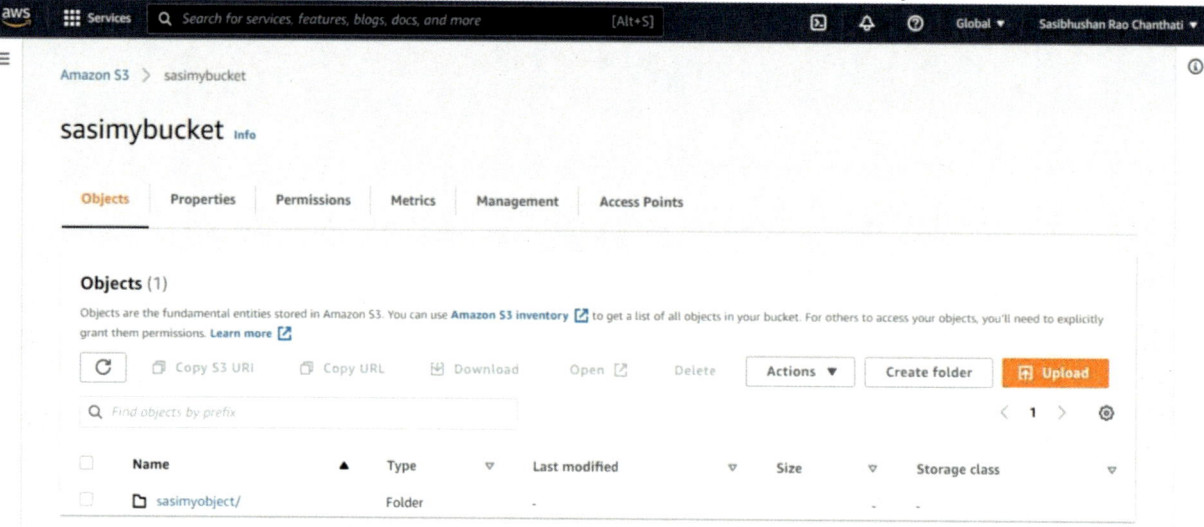

Permissions can be granted to the buckets – when user upload files to the buckets, for example we can make a public.

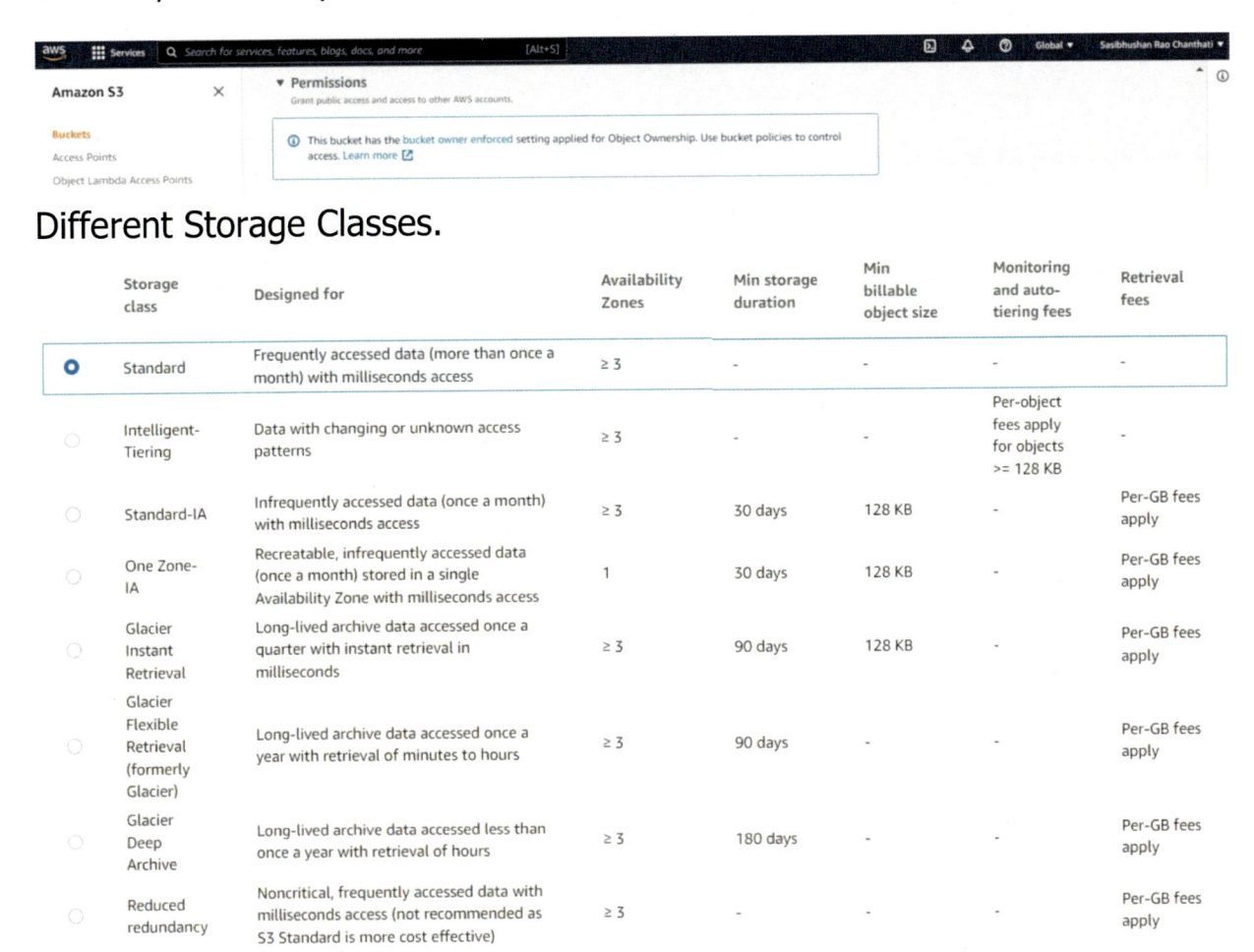

Different Storage Classes.

Storage class	Designed for	Availability Zones	Min storage duration	Min billable object size	Monitoring and auto-tiering fees	Retrieval fees
Standard	Frequently accessed data (more than once a month) with milliseconds access	≥ 3	-	-	-	-
Intelligent-Tiering	Data with changing or unknown access patterns	≥ 3	-	-	Per-object fees apply for objects >= 128 KB	-
Standard-IA	Infrequently accessed data (once a month) with milliseconds access	≥ 3	30 days	128 KB	-	Per-GB fees apply
One Zone-IA	Recreatable, infrequently accessed data (once a month) stored in a single Availability Zone with milliseconds access	1	30 days	128 KB	-	Per-GB fees apply
Glacier Instant Retrieval	Long-lived archive data accessed once a quarter with instant retrieval in milliseconds	≥ 3	90 days	128 KB	-	Per-GB fees apply
Glacier Flexible Retrieval (formerly Glacier)	Long-lived archive data accessed once a year with retrieval of minutes to hours	≥ 3	90 days	-	-	Per-GB fees apply
Glacier Deep Archive	Long-lived archive data accessed less than once a year with retrieval of hours	≥ 3	180 days	-	-	Per-GB fees apply
Reduced redundancy	Noncritical, frequently accessed data with milliseconds access (not recommended as S3 Standard is more cost effective)	≥ 3	-	-	-	Per-GB fees apply

Server-side encryption settings

Server-side encryption protects data at rest. Learn more 🗗

Server-side encryption
- ⦿ Do not specify an encryption key
- ○ Specify an encryption key

> ⚠ If your bucket policy requires encrypted uploads, you must specify an encryption key or your upload will fail.

> ⓘ Since default encryption is disabled for this bucket, no encryption settings will be applied to the objects when storing them in Amazon S3.

Tags - *optional*

Track storage cost or other criteria by tagging your objects. Learn more 🗗

No tags associated with this resource.

[Add tag]

Metadata - *optional*

Metadata is optional information provided as a name-value (key-value) pair. Learn more 🗗

No metadata associated with this resource.

[Add metadata]

Cancel   **Upload**

Bucket properties.

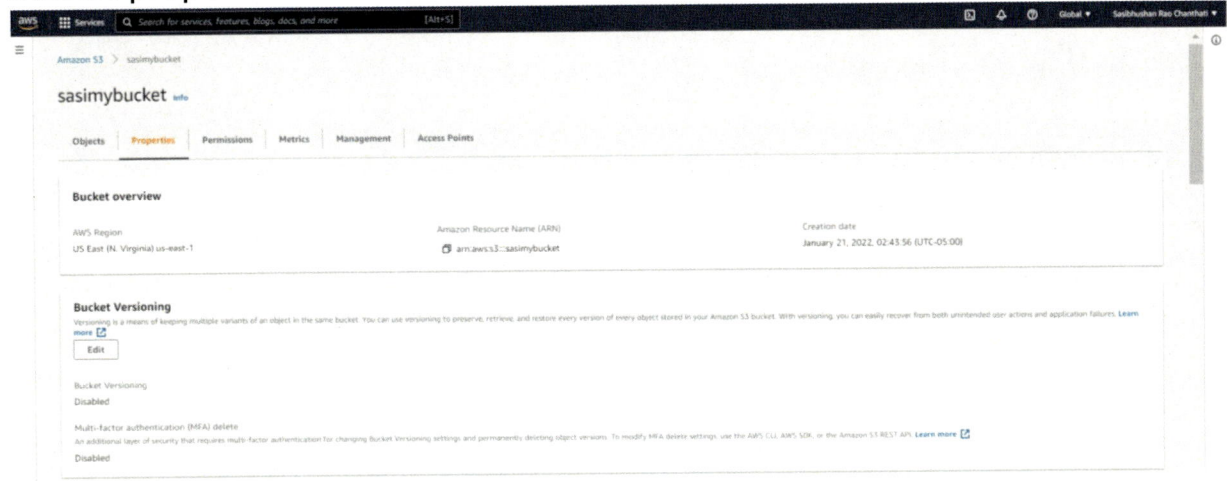

The bucket versioning can be enabled.

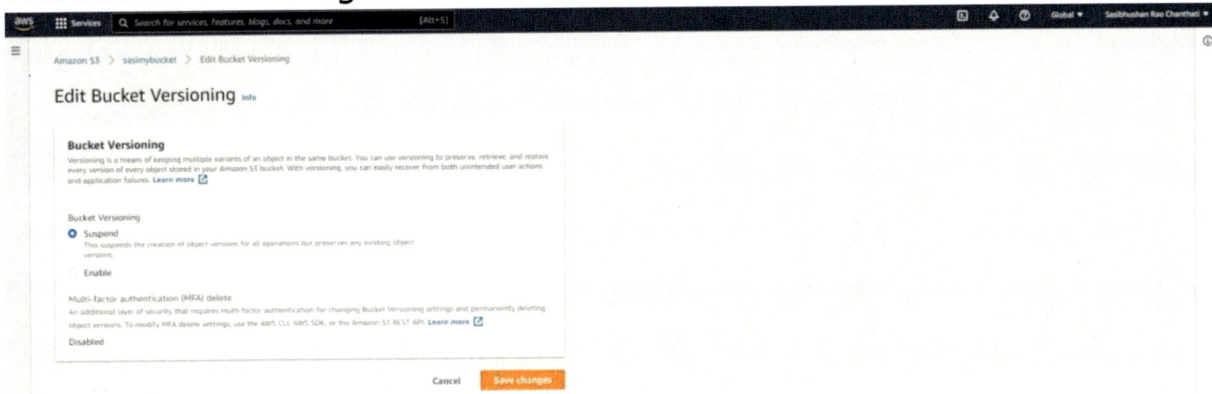

The default encryption will be always disabled.

Intelligent tiering configuration.

Amazon S3 > sasimybucket > Intelligent-Tiering Archive configurations >
Create Intelligent-Tiering Archive configuration

Create Intelligent-Tiering Archive configuration

Enable objects stored in the Intelligent-Tiering storage class to tier-down to the Archive Access tier or the Deep Archive Access tier which are optimized for objects that will be rarely accessed for long periods of time. Activate the Archive Access and Deep Archive Access tiers only if your objects can be accessed asynchronously by your application. Learn more

Archive configuration settings

Configuration name

[Enter configuration name]

The configuration name can contain up to 64 alphanumeric characters. You will not be able to change this name after the configuration has been created.

Choose a configuration scope

● Limit the scope of this configuration using one or more filters

○ This configuration applies to *all* objects in the bucket

Prefix
Add a filter to limit the scope of this configuration to a single prefix.

[Enter prefix]

Don't include the bucket name in the prefix. Using certain characters in key names can cause problems with some applications and protocols.

Object tags
You can limit the scope of this rule to the key value pairs added below.

[Add tag]

Status
Choose whether the configuration will be enabled or disabled.

○ Disable
● Enable

Archive rule actions

Intelligent-Tiering can tier down objects to the Archive Access tier, the Deep Archive Access tier, or both. The number of days until transition to the selected tiers can be extended up to a total of 2 years. Learn more

- [ ] **Archive Access tier**
  When enabled, Intelligent-Tiering will automatically move objects that haven't been accessed for a minimum of 90 days to the Archive Access tier.

- [ ] **Deep Archive Access tier**
  When enabled, Intelligent-Tiering will automatically move objects that haven't been accessed for a minimum of 180 days to the Deep Archive Access tier.

Cancel | **Create**

AWS CloudTrail data events | Configure in CloudTrail

Configure CloudTrail data events to log Amazon S3 object-level API operations in the CloudTrail console. Learn more

Name	Access

No data events
No data events to display.

Configure in CloudTrail

Event notifications (0) | Edit | Delete | Create event notification

Send a notification when specific events occur in your bucket. Learn more

Name	Event types	Filters	Destination type	Destination

No event notifications
Choose **Create event notification** to be notified when a specific event occurs.

Create event notification

Amazon EventBridge | Edit

For additional capabilities, use Amazon EventBridge to build event-driven applications at scale using S3 event notifications. Learn more or see EventBridge pricing

Send notifications to Amazon EventBridge for all events in this bucket
Off

Transfer acceleration
Use an accelerated endpoint for faster data transfers. Learn more

Transfer acceleration
Disabled

Object Lock
Store objects using a write-once-read-many (WORM) model to help you prevent objects from being deleted or overwritten for a fixed amount of time or indefinitely. Learn more

Object Lock
Disabled

ⓘ Amazon S3 currently does not support enabling Object Lock after a bucket has been created. To enable Object Lock for this bucket, contact Customer Support

Requester pays
When enabled, the requester pays for requests and data transfer costs, and anonymous access to this bucket is disabled. Learn more

Requester pays
Disabled

Static website hosting
Use this bucket to host a website or redirect requests. Learn more

Static website hosting
Disabled

S3 – Bucket Permissions

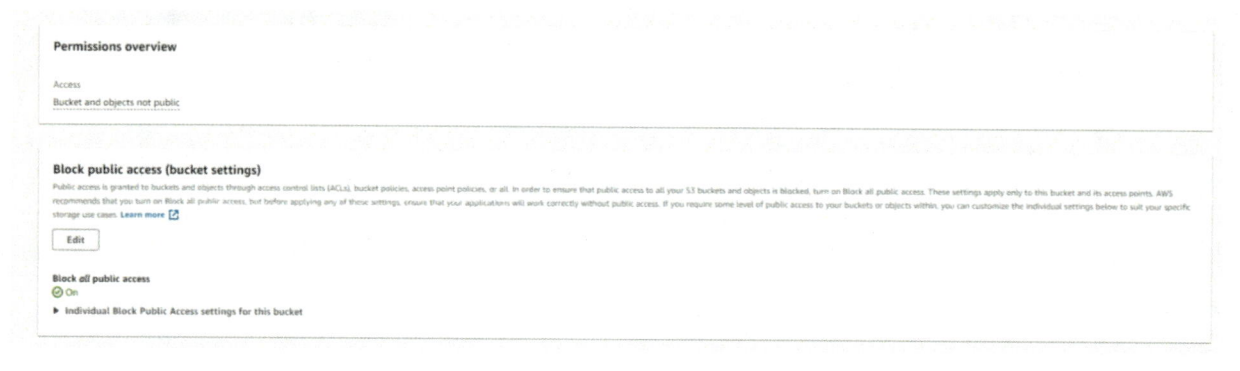

Permissions overview

Access
Bucket and objects not public

Block public access (bucket settings)
Public access is granted to buckets and objects through access control lists (ACLs), bucket policies, access point policies, or all. In order to ensure that public access to all your S3 buckets and objects is blocked, turn on Block all public access. These settings apply only to this bucket and its access points. AWS recommends that you turn on Block all public access, but before applying any of these settings, ensure that your applications will work correctly without public access. If you require some level of public access to your buckets or objects within, you can customize the individual settings below to suit your specific storage use cases. Learn more

[Edit]

Block all public access
⊘ On
▶ Individual Block Public Access settings for this bucket

S3 – Bucket Management and Life cycle rules:

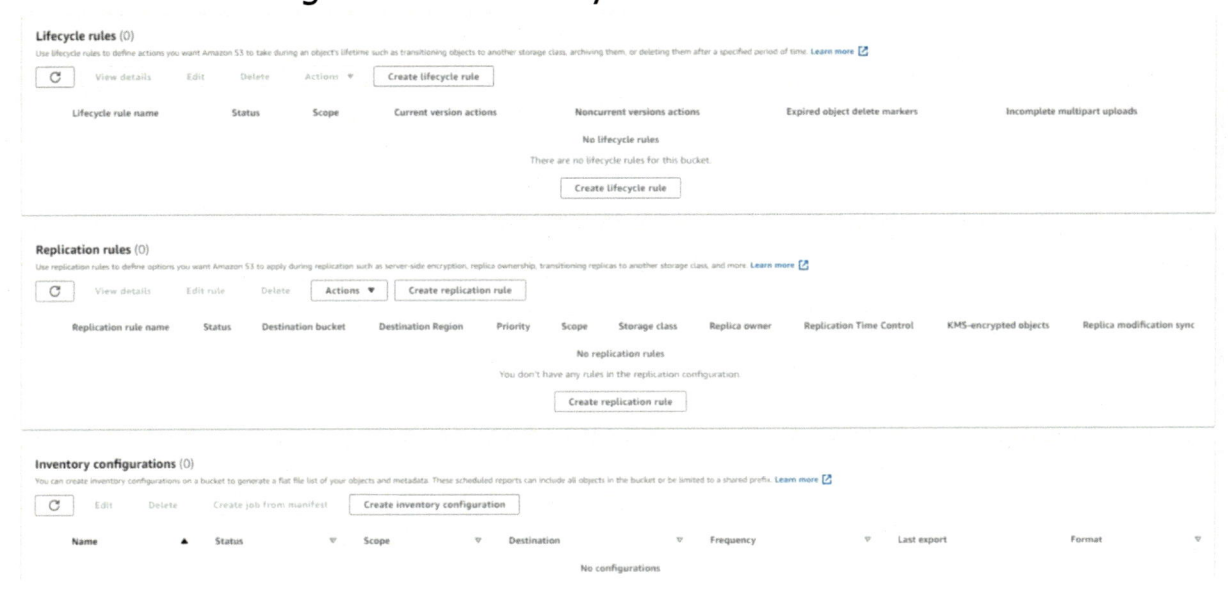

Lifecycle rules (0)
Use lifecycle rules to define actions you want Amazon S3 to take during an object's lifetime such as transitioning objects to another storage class, archiving them, or deleting them after a specified period of time. Learn more

Lifecycle rule name	Status	Scope	Current version actions	Noncurrent versions actions	Expired object delete markers	Incomplete multipart uploads

No lifecycle rules
There are no lifecycle rules for this bucket.

Create lifecycle rule

Replication rules (0)
Use replication rules to define options you want Amazon S3 to apply during replication such as server-side encryption, replica ownership, transitioning replicas to another storage class, and more. Learn more

Replication rule name	Status	Destination bucket	Destination Region	Priority	Scope	Storage class	Replica owner	Replication Time Control	KMS-encrypted objects	Replica modification sync

No replication rules
You don't have any rules in the replication configuration.

Create replication rule

Inventory configurations (0)
You can create inventory configurations on a bucket to generate a flat file list of your objects and metadata. These scheduled reports can include all objects in the bucket or be limited to a shared prefix. Learn more

Name	Status	Scope	Destination	Frequency	Last export	Format

No configurations

S3 – Bucket access points:

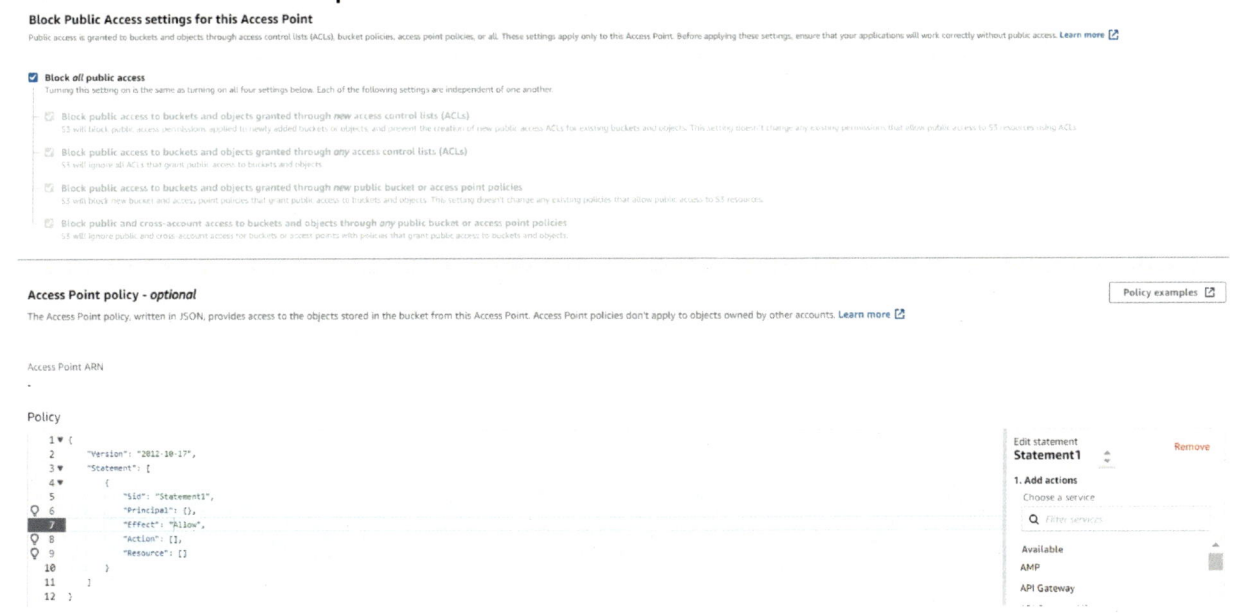

Block Public Access settings for this Access Point
Public access is granted to buckets and objects through access control lists (ACLs), bucket policies, access point policies, or all. These settings apply only to this Access Point. Before applying these settings, ensure that your applications will work correctly without public access. Learn more

☑ **Block all public access**
Turning this setting on is the same as turning on all four settings below. Each of the following settings are independent of one another.

☐ Block public access to buckets and objects granted through *new* access control lists (ACLs)
S3 will block public access permissions applied to newly added buckets or objects, and prevent the creation of new public access ACLs for existing buckets and objects. This setting doesn't change any existing permissions that allow public access to S3 resources using ACLs.

☑ Block public access to buckets and objects granted through *any* access control lists (ACLs)
S3 will ignore all ACLs that grant public access to buckets and objects.

☐ Block public access to buckets and objects granted through *new* public bucket or access point policies
S3 will block new bucket and access point policies that grant public access to buckets and objects. This setting doesn't change any existing policies that allow public access to S3 resources.

☐ Block public and cross-account access to buckets and objects through *any* public bucket or access point policies
S3 will ignore public and cross-account access for buckets or access points with policies that grant public access to buckets and objects.

Access Point policy - *optional*
The Access Point policy, written in JSON, provides access to the objects stored in the bucket from this Access Point. Access Point policies don't apply to objects owned by other accounts. Learn more

Policy examples

Access Point ARN

Policy
```
 1  {
 2      "Version": "2012-10-17",
 3      "Statement": [
 4          {
 5              "Sid": "Statement1",
 6              "Principal": {},
 7              "Effect": "Allow",
 8              "Action": [],
 9              "Resource": []
10          }
11      ]
12  }
```

Edit statement
Statement1   Remove

1. Add actions
   Choose a service
   🔍 Filter services

   Available
   AMP
   API Gateway

Use Case: Managing the AWS S3 objects and bucket using AWS CLI V2 – Windows

Overview:

In this use case, we will be loading/deleting images, documents (word, PDF, excel), videos to S3 buckets by creating objects using AWS S3 CLI V2. First step is the Installation of CLI and connecting it to the AWS console using access keys, this can be installed on any system, use the below URL for complete documents. Once the download of the installer is completed and installation is completed. Open command prompt and follow the below steps. https://aws.amazon.com/cli/

To check the version type aws --version in the command prompt

```
C:\Users\sasibh>aws --version
aws-cli/2.4.12 Python/3.8.8 Windows/10 exe/AMD64 prompt/off

C:\Users\sasibh>
```

AWS CLI basic structure – Command, sub command and parameters.

```
$ aws <command> <subcommand> [options and parameters]
```

Once the installation is done, check the security credentials.

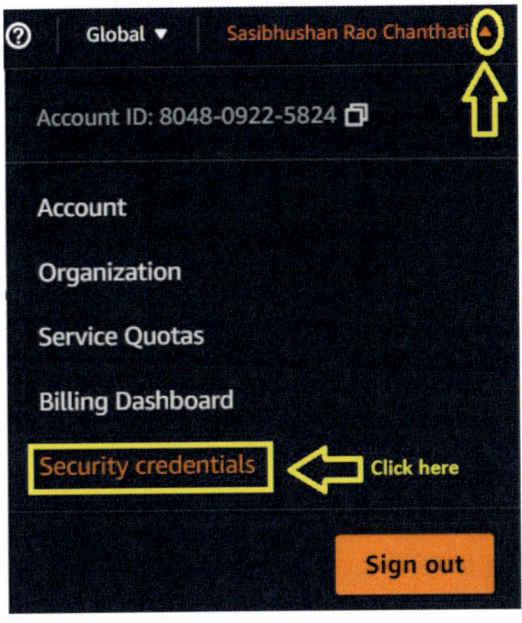

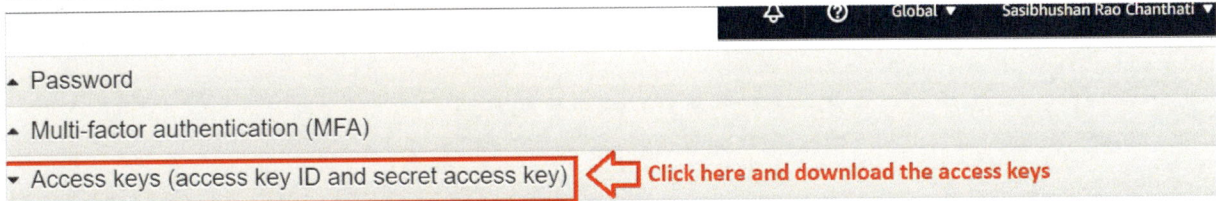

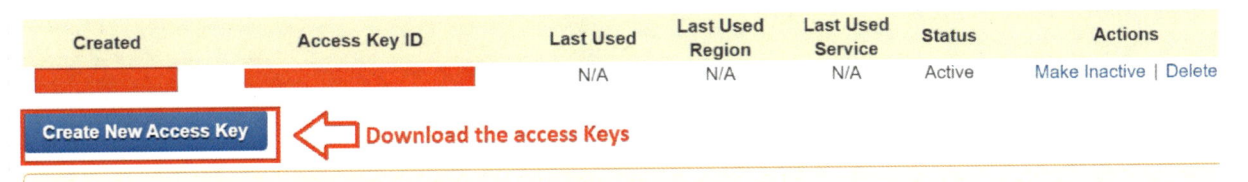

Once the access keys are downloaded – go to command prompt and configure them. For region check here:

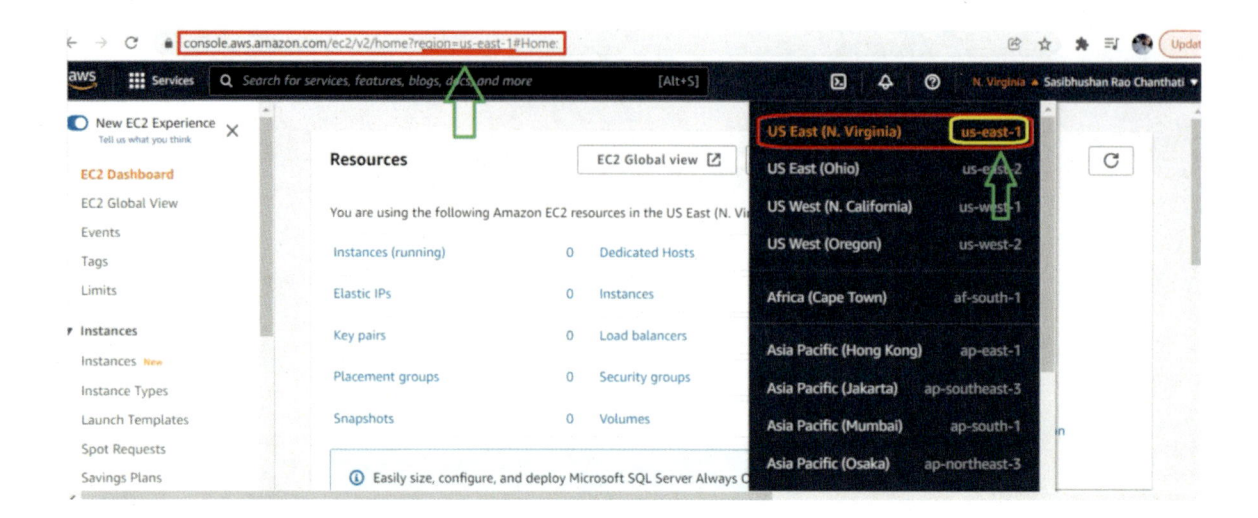

Check your default output formats:

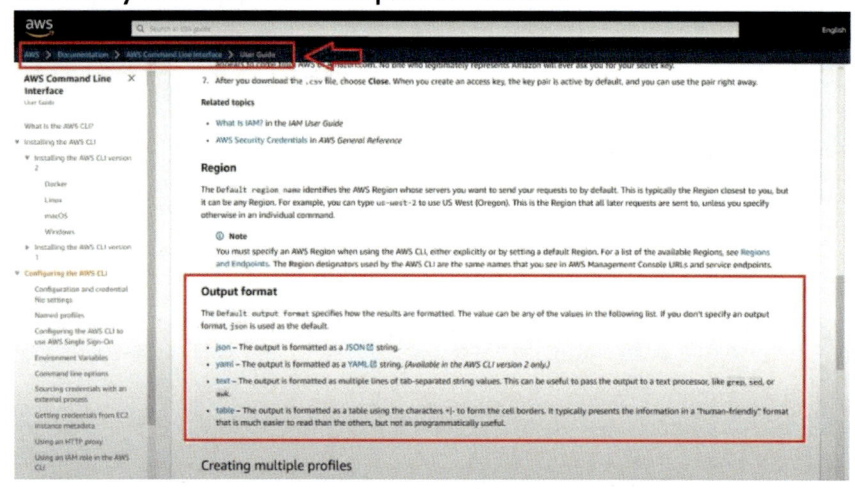

aws configure, enter the access key, access secret, region name and output format.

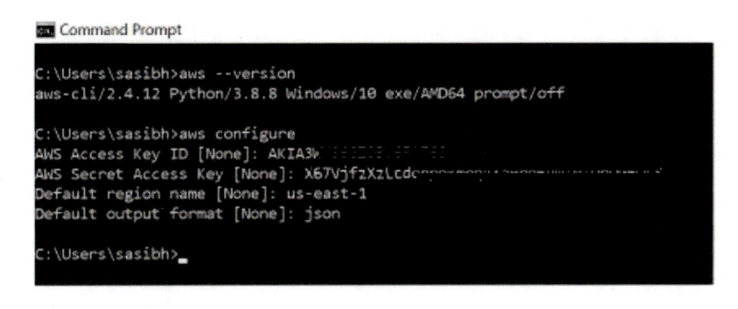

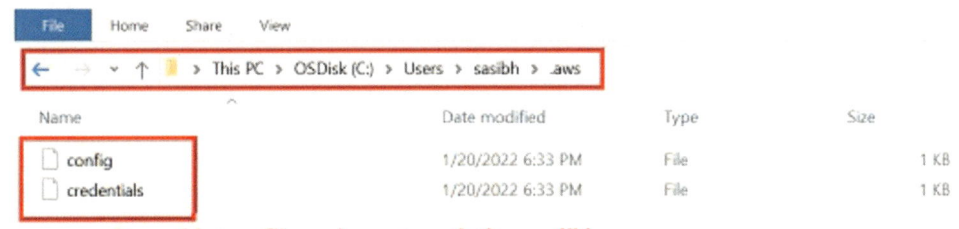

```
C:\Users\sasibh>aws --version
aws-cli/2.4.12 Python/3.8.8 Windows/10 exe/AMD64 prompt/off

C:\Users\sasibh>aws configure
AWS Access Key ID [None]: AKIA3...
AWS Secret Access Key [None]: X67VjfzXzLcd...
Default region name [None]: us-east-1
Default output format [None]: json

C:\Users\sasibh>
```

Path: This PC > OSDisk (C:) > Users > sasibh > .aws

Name	Date modified	Type	Size
config	1/20/2022 6:33 PM	File	1 KB
credentials	1/20/2022 6:33 PM	File	1 KB

Open this two files using notepad, these will be stored .aws folder

Useful Information for AWS CLI – S3

To get latest information on AWS S3 – Type "aws s3 help" in the command prompt as shown below.

```
Command Prompt - aws s3 help
Microsoft Windows [Version 10.0.19041.1415]
(c) Microsoft Corporation. All rights reserved.

C:\Users\sasibh>aws s3 help
```

S3 description:

This section explains prominent concepts and notations in the set of high-level S3 commands provided.

Whenever using a command, at least one path argument must be specified. There are two types of path arguments: "LocalPath" and "S3Uri". "LocalPath": represents the path of a local file or directory. It can be written as an absolute path or relative path. "S3Uri": represents the location of a S3 object, prefix, or bucket.

This must be written in the form "s3://mybucket/mykey" where "mybucket" is the specified S3 bucket, "mykey" is the specified S3 key. The path argument must begin with "s3://" to denote that the path argument refers to a S3 object.

Note that prefixes are separated by forward slashes. For example, if the S3 object "myobject" had the prefix "myprefix", the S3 key would be "myprefix/myobject", and if the object was in the bucket "mybucket", the "S3Uri" would be "s3://mybucket/myprefix/myobject". "S3Uri" also supports S3 access points.

To specify an access point, this value must be of the form "s3://<access-point-arn>/<key>". For example, if the access point "myaccesspoint" to be used has the ARN: "arn:aws:s3:uswest-2:123456789012:accesspoint/myaccesspoint" and the object being accessed has the key "mykey", then the "S3URI" used must be: "s3://arn:aws:s3:us-west2:123456789012:accesspoint/myaccesspoint/mykey". Like bucket names, you can also use prefixes with access point ARNs for the "S3Uri". For example: "s3://arn:aws:s3:us-west-2:123456789012:accesspoint/myaccesspoint/myprefix/". The higher level "s3" commands do **not** support access point object ARNs. For example, if the following was specified: "s3://arn:aws:s3:us-west-2:123456789012:accesspoint/myaccesspoint/object/mykey" the "S3URI" will resolve to the object key "object/mykey".

Order of Path Arguments, every command takes one or two positional path arguments. The first path argument represents the source, which is the local file/directory or S3 object/prefix/bucket that is being referenced. If there is a second path argument, it represents the destination, which is the local file/directory or S3 object/prefix/bucket that is being operated on.

Commands with only one path argument do not have a destination because the operation is being performed only on the source. Single Local file and S3 Object Operations.

Some commands perform operations only on single files and S3 objects. The following commands are single file/object operations if no "-- recursive" flag is provided.   * "cp"
"mv"
"rm"

For this type of operation, the first path argument, the source, must exist and be a local file or S3 object. The second path argument, the destination, can be the name of a local file, local directory, S3 object, S3 prefix, or S3 bucket.

The destination is indicated as a local directory, S3 prefix, or S3 bucket if it ends with a forward slash or back slash. The use of slash depends on the path argument type. If the path argument is a "LocalPath", the type of slash is the separator used by the operating system. If the path is a "S3Uri", the forward slash must always be used. If a slash is at the end of the destination, the destination file or object will adopt the name of the source file or object.

Otherwise, if there is no slash at the end, the file or object will be saved under the name provided. See examples in "cp" and "mv" to illustrate this description.

Directory and S3 Prefix Operations: Some commands only perform operations on the contents of a local directory or S3 prefix/bucket. Adding or omitting a forward slash or back slash to the end of any path argument, depending on its type, does not affect the results of the operation.

The following commands will always result in a directory or S3 prefix/bucket operation:
"sync"
"mb"
"rb"
"ls"

Use of Exclude and Include Filters:
Currently, there is no support for the use of UNIX style wildcards in a command's path arguments. However, most commands have "--exclude"<value>"" and "--include "<value>"" parameters that can achieve the desired result. These parameters perform pattern matching to either exclude or include a particular file or object.
The following pattern symbols are supported.
"*": Matches everything
"?": Matches any single character
"[sequence]": Matches any character in "sequence"
"[!sequence]": Matches any character not in "sequence"
Any number of these parameters can be passed to a command. You can do this by providing an "--exclude" or "--include" argument multiple times, e.g. "-include "*.txt" --include "*.png"".
When there are multiple filters, the rule is the filters that appear later in the command take precedence over filters that appear earlier in the command. For example, if the filter parameters passed to the command were   --exclude "*" --include "*.txt".
All files will be excluded from the command except for files ending with ".txt"
However, if the order of the filter parameters was changed to
   --include "*.txt" --exclude "*"
All files will be excluded from the command. Each filter is evaluated against the **source directory**. If the source location is a file instead of a directory, the directory containing

the file is used as the source directory. For example, suppose you had the following directory structure:
   /tmp/foo/
     .git/
     |---config
     |--description   foo.txt   bar.txt   baz.jpg

In the command "aws s3 sync /tmp/foo s3://bucket/" the source directory is "/tmp/foo". Any include/exclude filters will be evaluated with the source directory prepended. Below are several examples to demonstrate this.

Given the directory structure above and the command "aws s3 cp/tmp/foo s3://bucket/ -recursive --exclude ".git/*"", the files ".git/config" and ".git/description" will be excluded from the files to upload because the exclude filter ".git/*" will have the source prepended to the filter. This means that:
   /tmp/foo/.git/* -> /tmp/foo/.git/config (matches, should exclude)
   /tmp/foo/.git/* -> /tmp/foo/.git/description (matches, should exclude)
   /tmp/foo/.git/* -> /tmp/foo/foo.txt (does not match, should include)
   /tmp/foo/.git/* -> /tmp/foo/bar.txt (does not match, should include)
   /tmp/foo/.git/* -> /tmp/foo/baz.jpg (does not match, should include)

The command "aws s3 cp /tmp/foo/ s3://bucket/ --recursive --exclude

"ba*"" will exclude "/tmp/foo/bar.txt" and "/tmp/foo/baz.jpg":
   /tmp/foo/ba* -> /tmp/foo/.git/config (does not match, should include)
   /tmp/foo/ba* -> /tmp/foo/.git/description (does not match, should include)
   /tmp/foo/ba* -> /tmp/foo/foo.txt (does not match, should include)

/tmp/foo/ba* -> /tmp/foo/bar.txt (matches, should exclude)
/tmp/foo/ba* -> /tmp/foo/baz.jpg (matches, should exclude)

Note that, by default, *all files are included*. This means that providing **only** an "-include" filter will not change what files are transferred. "--include" will only re-include files that have been excluded from an "--exclude" filter.

If you only want to upload files with a particular extension, you need to first exclude all files, then re-include the files with the extension. This command will upload **only** files ending with ".jpg":

aws s3 cp /tmp/foo/ s3://bucket/ --recursive --exclude "*" --include "*.jpg" If you wanted to include both ".jpg" files as well as ".txt" files you can run:

   aws s3 cp /tmp/foo/ s3://bucket/ --recursive \
  --exclude "*" --include "*.jpg" --include "*.txt"

Use Case: REST Integration using AWS Glue ETL job (API as source end point and destination as AWS S3)

In this use case, the AWS Glue job will communicate with public REST API, which is hosted in a web app, which will make call to API and post the data into S3 bucket.

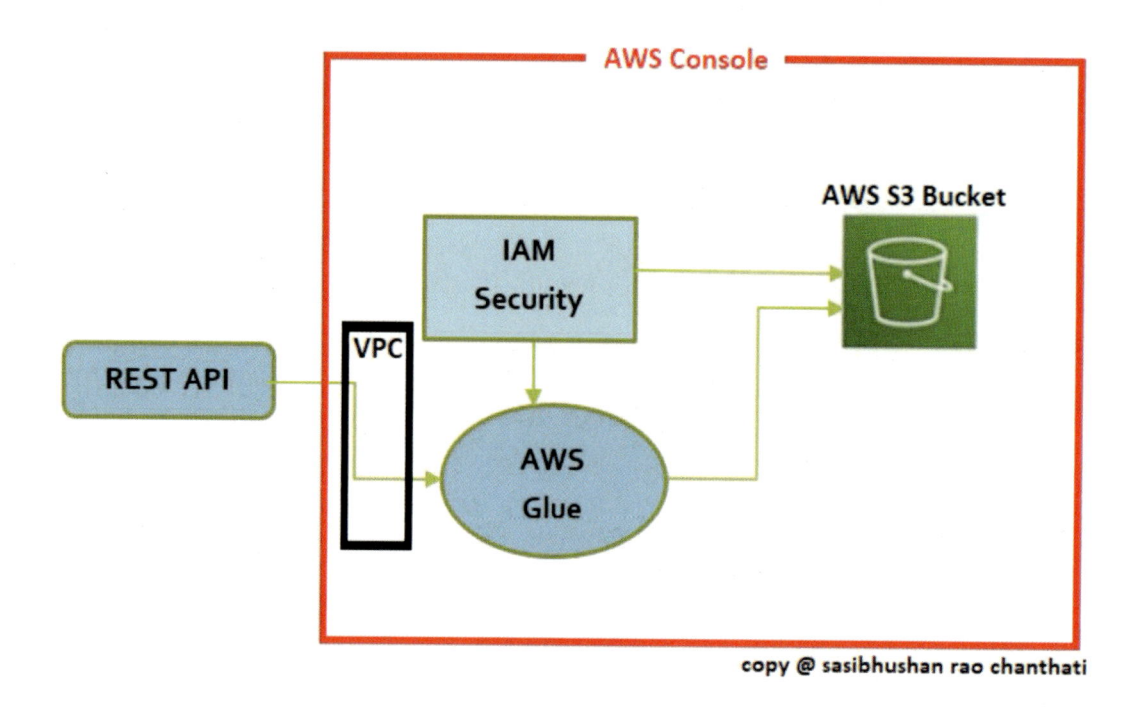

copy @ sasibhushan rao chanthati

To make the communication between REST API and Glue Job we will create VPC with private subnet which will have Network Access Control (NAC) gateway configured to make an outbound call, an EIN is created in the private subnet for making the outbound call.

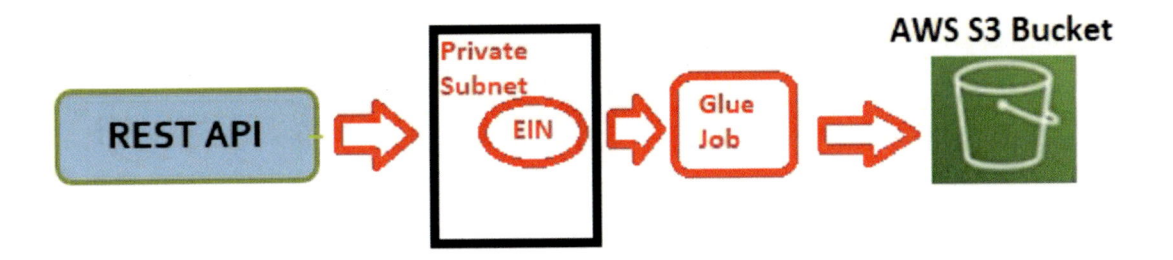

REST API ⇒ Private Subnet (ENI) ⇒ Glue Job ⇒ AWS S3 Bucket

VPC creation – both pivate setnet and public subnet. VPC is required, because the AWS Glue Job needs an AWS Elastic network interfaces (ENI) to call the REST API over web. The ENI is created in the private subnet with NATGateway (Network Address Translation) using AWS Glue connection. NAT Gateway will enable outbound call to the REST API.

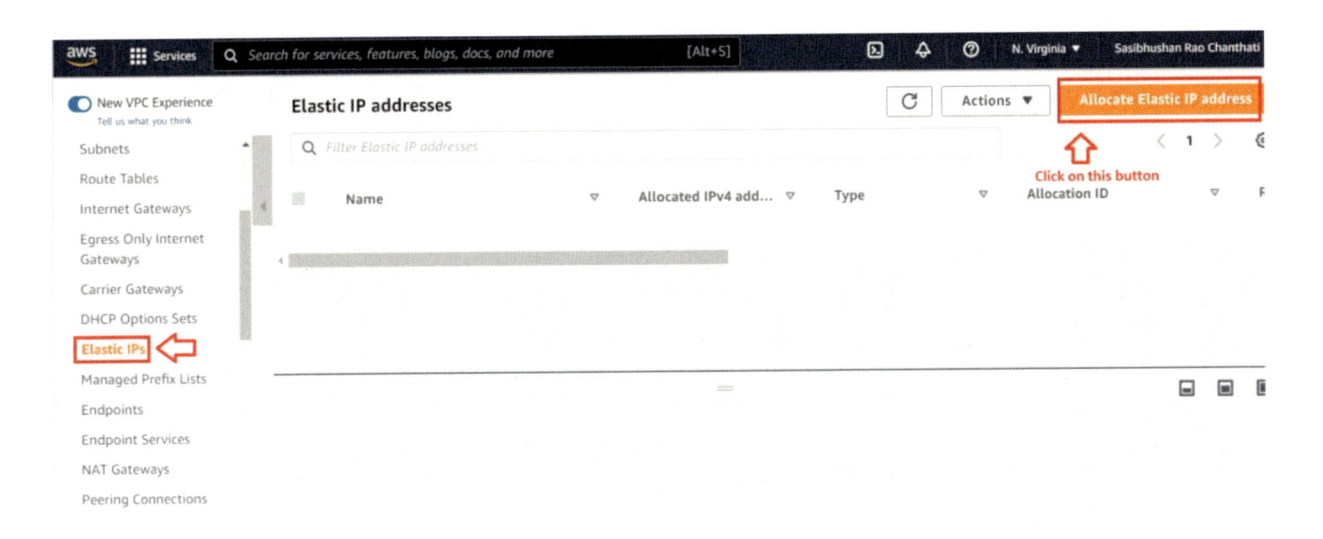

Allocate Elastic IP address Info

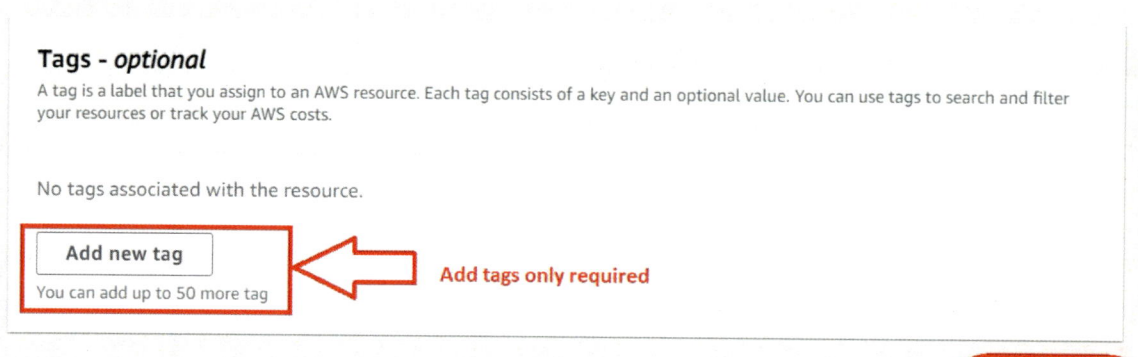

Elastic IP address settings Info

Network Border Group Info

🔍 us-east-1   ✕

Public IPv4 address pool

● Amazon's pool of IPv4 addresses

○ Public IPv4 address that you bring to your AWS account (option disabled because no pools found) Learn more 🔗

○ Customer owned pool of IPv4 addresses (option disabled because no customer owned pools found) Learn more 🔗

Global static IP addresses

AWS Global Accelerator can provide global static IP addresses that are announced worldwide using anycast from AWS edge locations. This can help improve the availability and latency for your user traffic by using the Amazon global network. Learn more 🔗

[Create accelerator 🔗]

Tags - *optional*

A tag is a label that you assign to an AWS resource. Each tag consists of a key and an optional value. You can use tags to search and filter your resources or track your AWS costs.

No tags associated with the resource.

[**Add new tag**] ⟵ **Add tags only required**
You can add up to 50 more tag

Cancel   [**Allocate**]

Click here

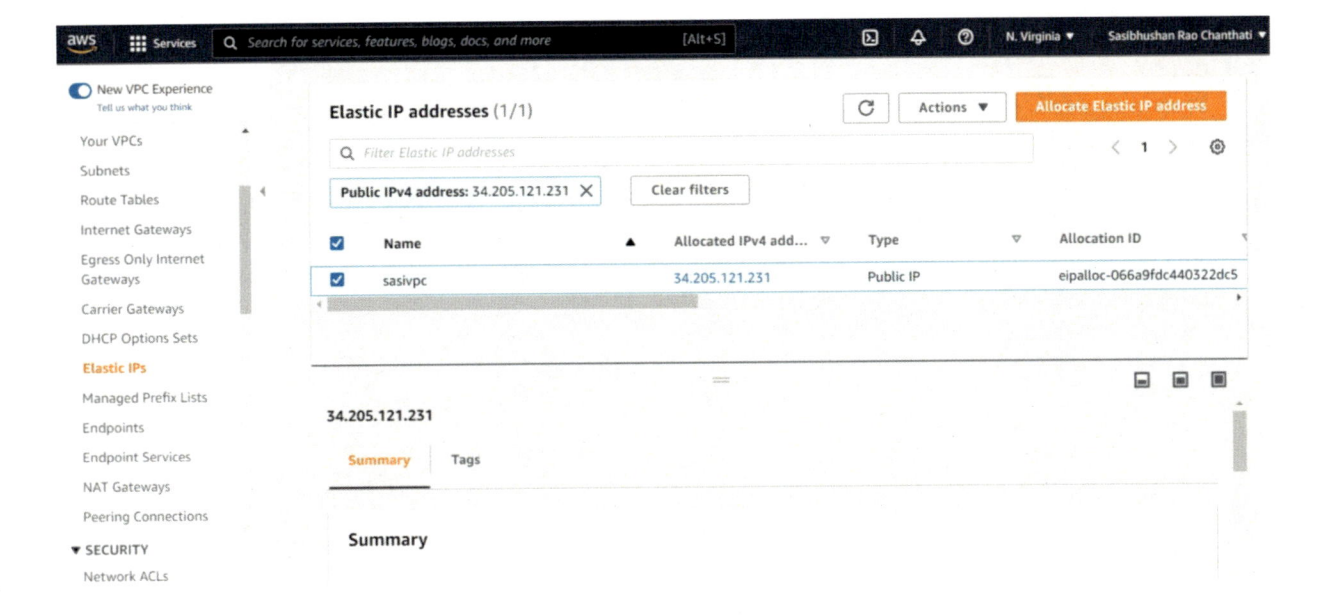

Create role using IAM:

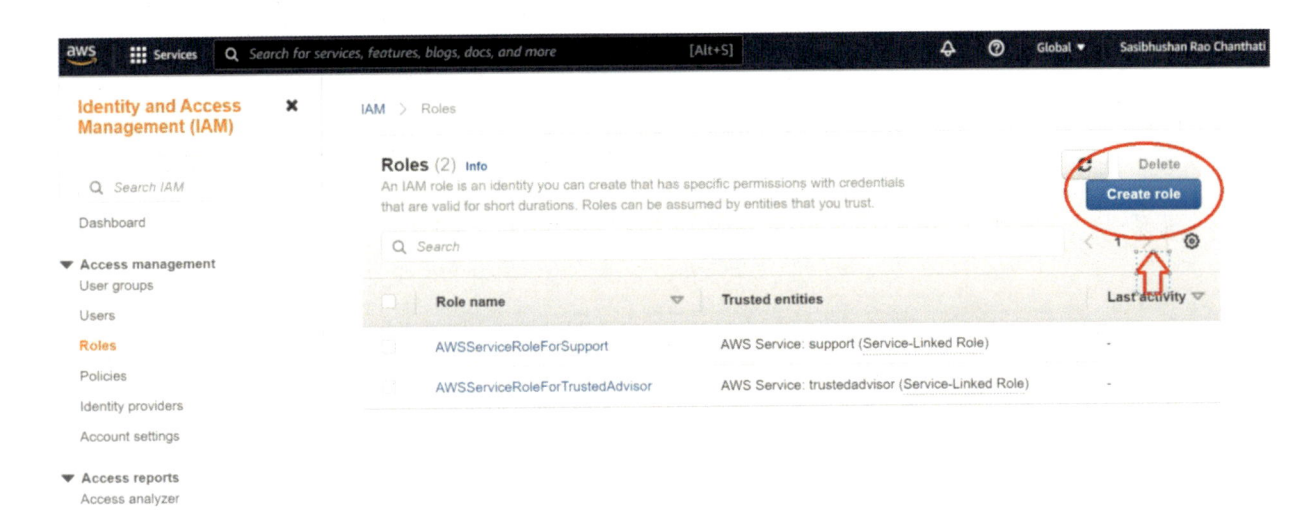

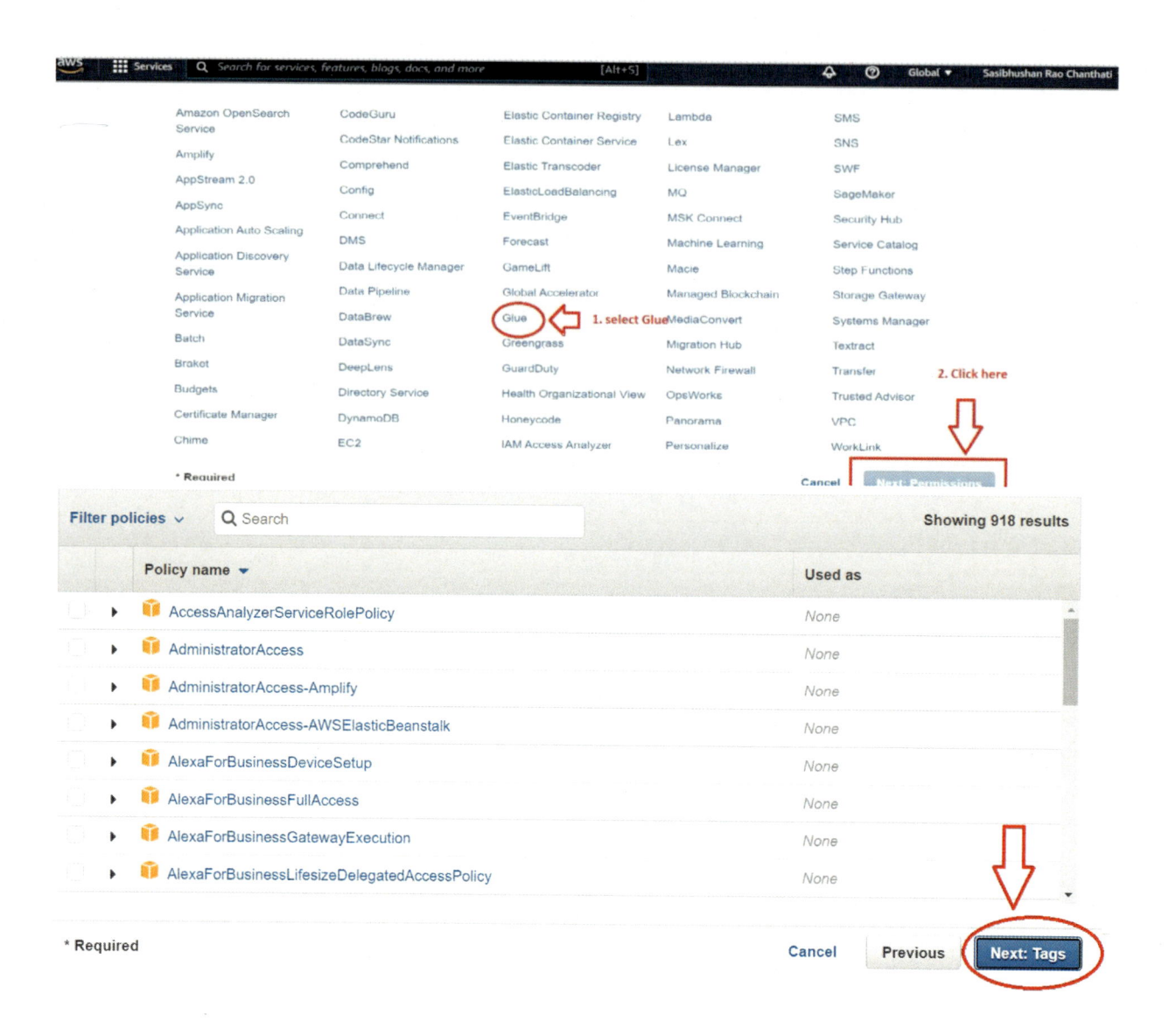

Amazon OpenSearch Service	CodeGuru	Elastic Container Registry	Lambda	SMS
Amplify	CodeStar Notifications	Elastic Container Service	Lex	SNS
AppStream 2.0	Comprehend	Elastic Transcoder	License Manager	SWF
AppSync	Config	ElasticLoadBalancing	MQ	SageMaker
Application Auto Scaling	Connect	EventBridge	MSK Connect	Security Hub
Application Discovery Service	DMS	Forecast	Machine Learning	Service Catalog
Application Migration Service	Data Lifecycle Manager	GameLift	Macie	Step Functions
Batch	Data Pipeline	Global Accelerator	Managed Blockchain	Storage Gateway
Brakot	DataBrew	Glue ⇐ 1. select Glue	MediaConvert	Systems Manager
Budgets	DataSync	Greengrass	Migration Hub	Textract
Certificate Manager	DeepLens	GuardDuty	Network Firewall	Transfer 2. Click here
Chime	Directory Service	Health Organizational View	OpsWorks	Trusted Advisor
	DynamoDB	Honeycode	Panorama	VPC
	EC2	IAM Access Analyzer	Personalize	WorkLink

*Required   Cancel   **Next: Permissions**

Filter policies ▾   🔍 Search   Showing 918 results

	Policy name ▾	Used as
▸	📦 AccessAnalyzerServiceRolePolicy	None
▸	📦 AdministratorAccess	None
▸	📦 AdministratorAccess-Amplify	None
▸	📦 AdministratorAccess-AWSElasticBeanstalk	None
▸	📦 AlexaForBusinessDeviceSetup	None
▸	📦 AlexaForBusinessFullAccess	None
▸	📦 AlexaForBusinessGatewayExecution	None
▸	📦 AlexaForBusinessLifesizeDelegatedAccessPolicy	None

*Required   Cancel   Previous   **Next: Tags**

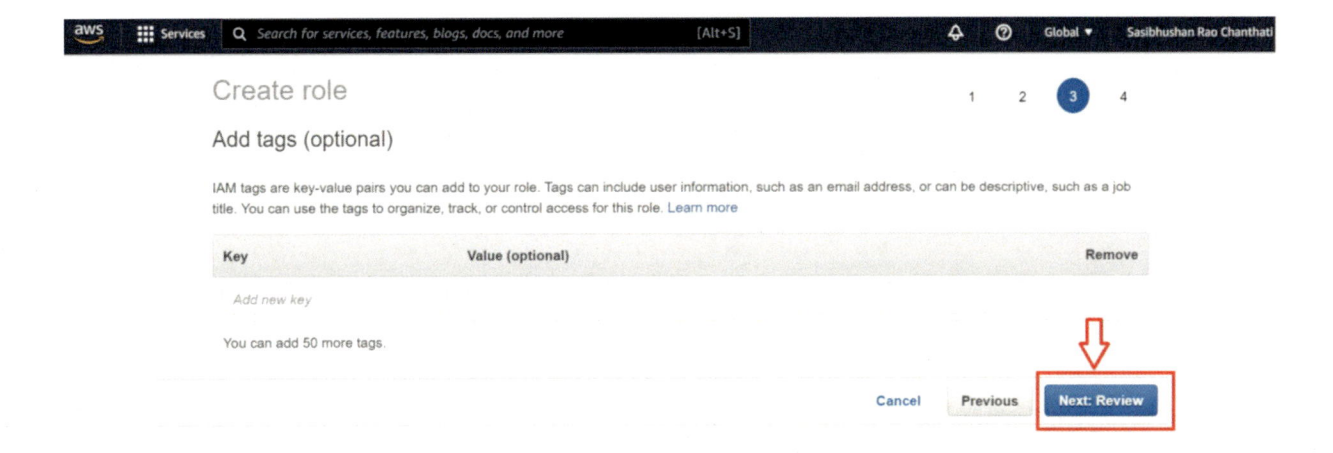

Creation of AWS Glue connection. The connection is used to create an ENI in the private subnet of the VPC. AWS Glue job uses ENI to make call to the internet-based REST API. It is a dummy connection with sole purpose to create an ENI for the AWS Glue Job.

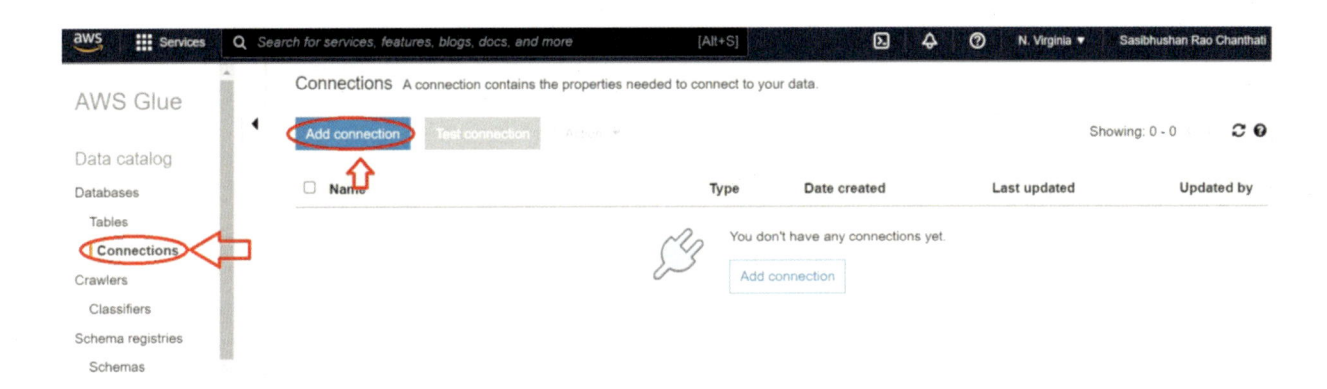

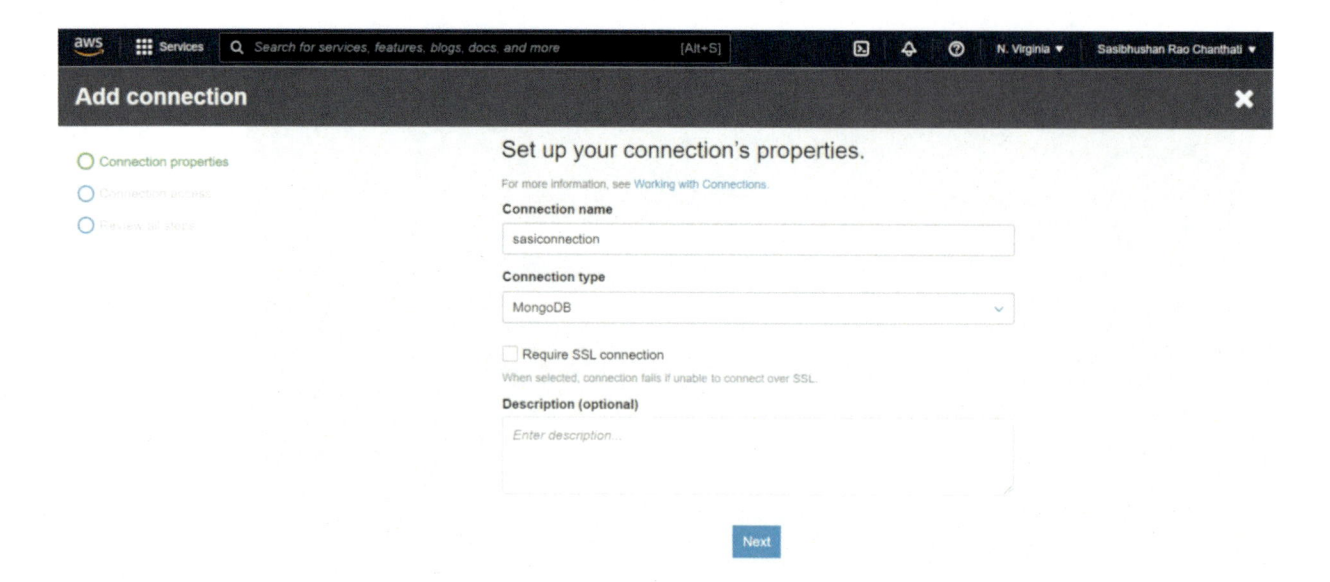

Create the AWS Glue job which calls the REST API and copies the output data in the Amazon S3 bucket. In AWS Glue – add job,

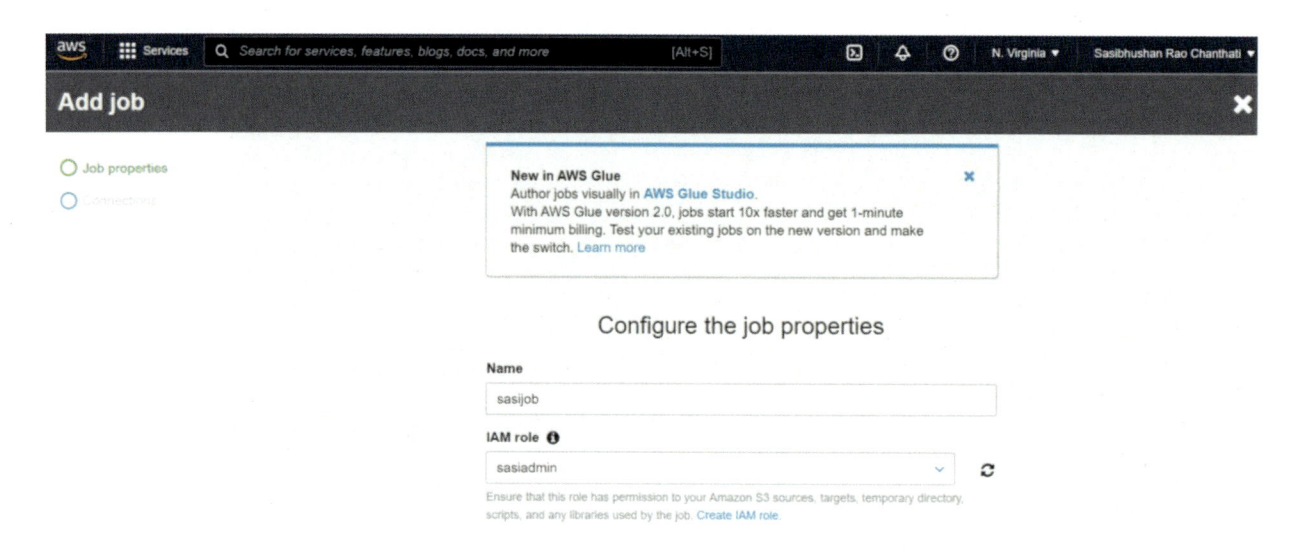

Add job

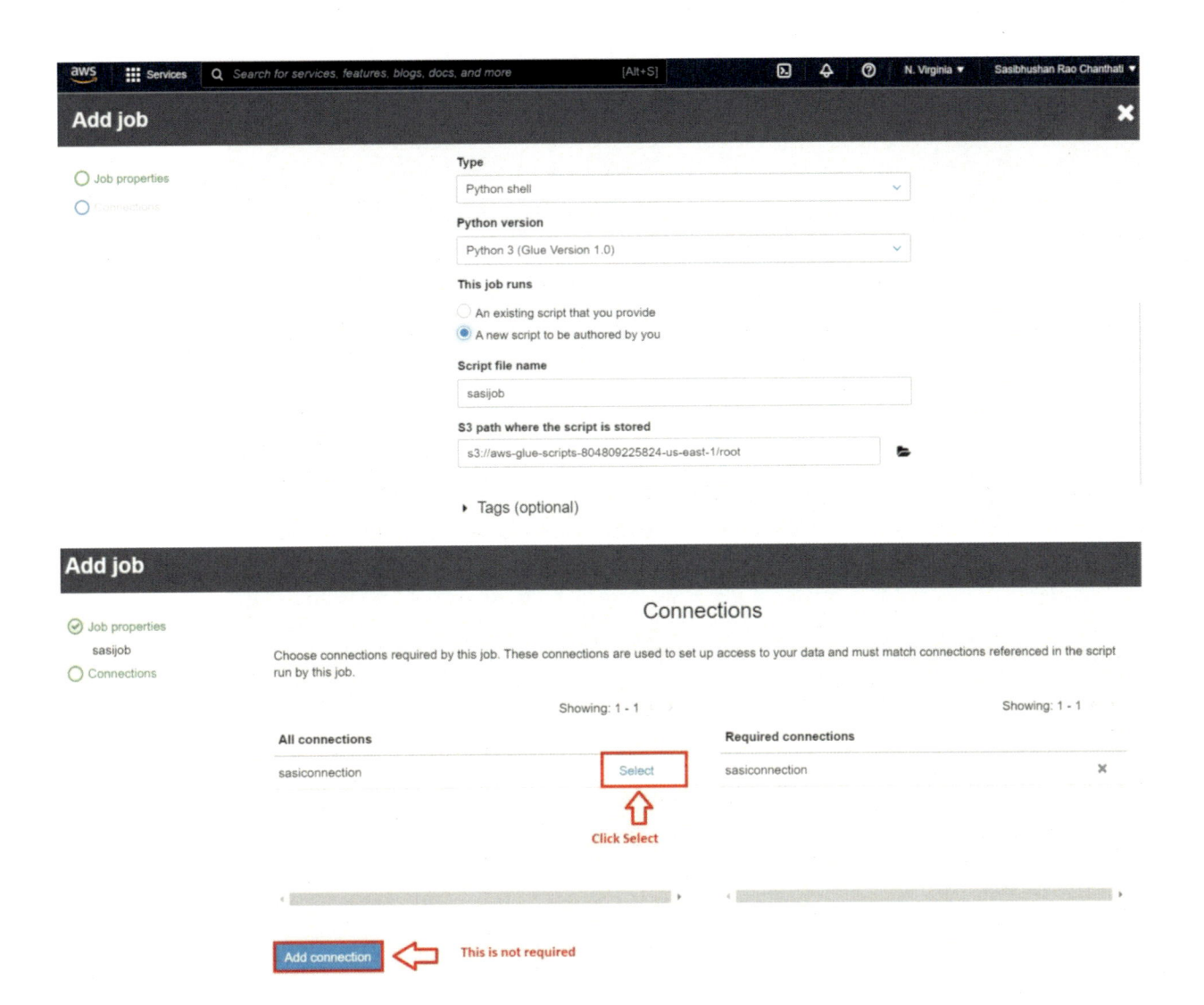

- ⊙ Job properties
- ○ Connections

Type

Python shell

Python version

Python 3 (Glue Version 1.0)

This job runs

○ An existing script that you provide
● A new script to be authored by you

Script file name

sasijob

S3 path where the script is stored

s3://aws-glue-scripts-804809225824-us-east-1/root

▸ Tags (optional)

Add job

- ✓ Job properties
  - sasijob
- ○ Connections

Connections

Choose connections required by this job. These connections are used to set up access to your data and must match connections referenced in the script run by this job.

Showing: 1 - 1

All connections

sasiconnection   Select

⇧ **Click Select**

Showing: 1 - 1

Required connections

sasiconnection   ✕

Add connection ⇐ **This is not required**

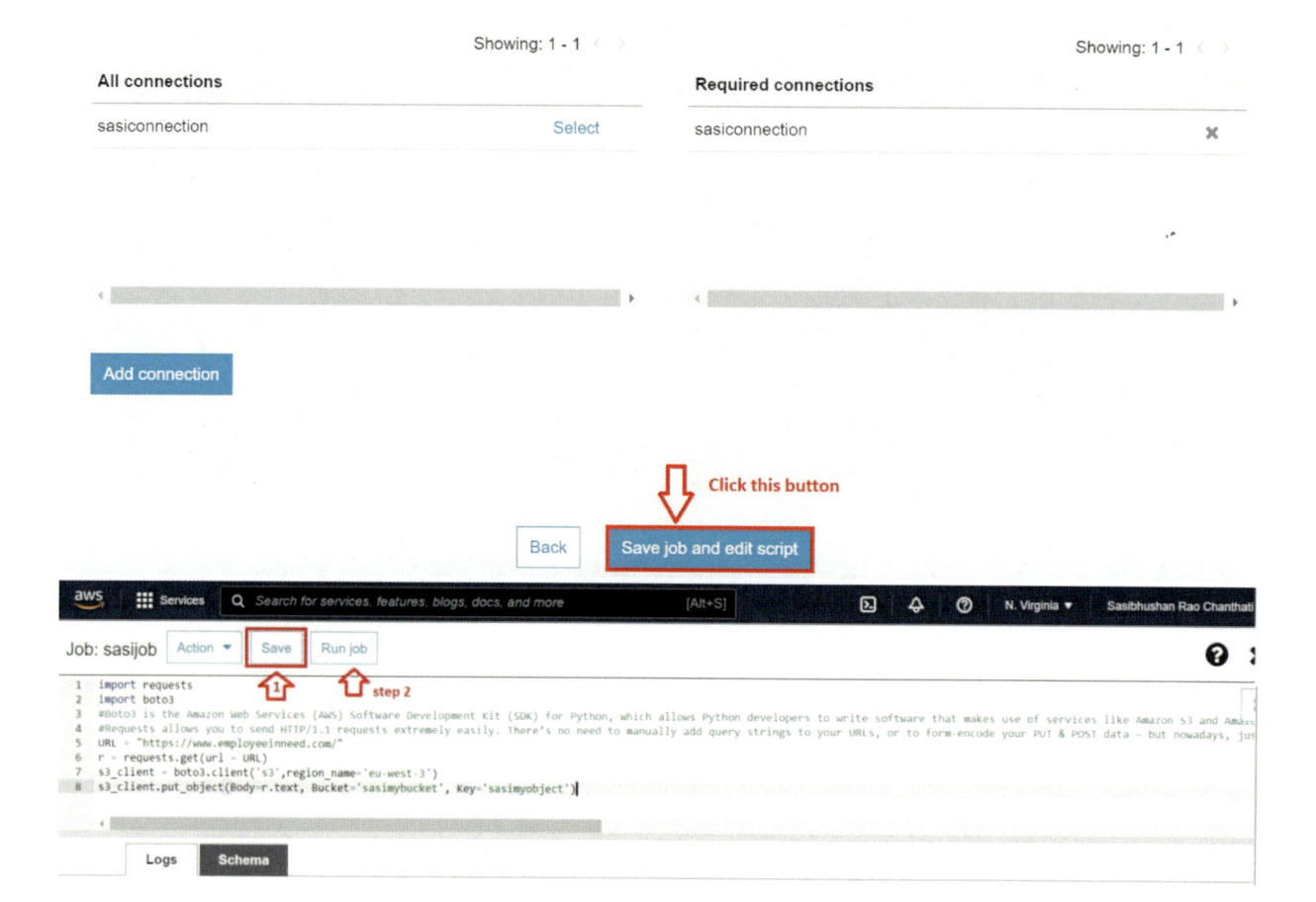

import
requests
import
boto3
#Boto3 is the Amazon Web Services (AWS) Software Development Kit (SDK) for Python, which allows Python developers to write software that makes use of services like Amazon S3 and Amazon EC2.
#Requests allows you to send HTTP/1.1 requests extremely easily. There's no need to manually add query strings to your URLs, or to form-encode your PUT & POST data — but nowadays, just use the json method! Requests is one of the most downloaded Python packages today, pulling in around 30M downloads / week— according to GitHub, Requests is currently

depended upon by 1,000,000+ repositories. You may certainly put your trust in this code

URL = " https://www.employeeinneed.com/"
# above is dummy URL of API, logic to load data in object for specfic bucket r = requests.get(url = URL)
s3_client = boto3.client('s3',region_name='eu-west-3') s3_client.put_object(Body=r.text, Bucket='sasimybucket', Key='sasimyobject')

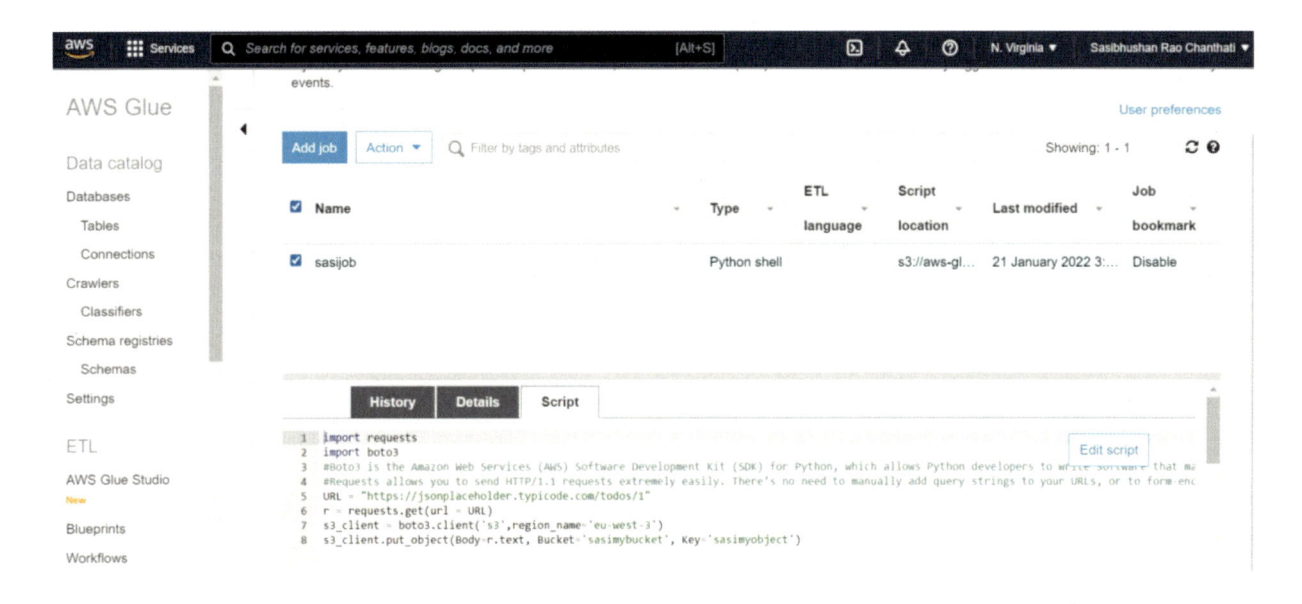

Benefits of Cloud Migration

There might be some challenges and potential risks during cloud migration. But that shouldn't deter any financial organization from migrating to a cloud. Because even with the risks, once done successfully and carefully, this change involves many benefits.

1. Enterprise synchronization

Cloud adoption allows various business units to be integrated under a unified platform. This integration enables data sharing among teams, better collaboration, improve decision-making processes, provide analytics and insights, and more.

2. IT security

Security in cloud computing is not just a challenge but a benefit as well. The data remains secure even when there is a server crash. Security mechanisms like firewalls not only stop malware and viruses but data theft as well.

3. Business agility

Going cloud improves resilience and agility. Since data and services are readily available, it increases the business's efficiency as the information is available at their fingertips for both the employees and customers. Cloud platforms enable advanced delivery techniques, including Continuous Integration and DevOps, to ensure that your service delivery is optimally efficient.

Along with agility, cloud infrastructure also increases operational efficiencies and facilitates growth. For example, Square 1 Bank's cloud presence had reduced its average time to close a loan by more than 20 percent with the cloud migration.[10]

Many cloud service providers offer an operation-based pricing mechanism or popularly known as pay-as-you-go. This pricing strategy enables the industries to scale computing costs and responds to shifts and changes in market dynamics, which is very common in financial sectors.

5. Reduced costs of maintenance

With less physical architecture, the day-to-day maintenance is significantly reduced. Costs like procuring software, storing, and maintaining multiple servers, equipment, and other hardware are greatly reduced.

6. Enhanced customer and employee experience

Cloud service providers usually offer AI tools that improve customer service and streamline operations. With analytics tools providing insights into customer behavior, customer experience can be improved by personalization.

To cater to the needs of millions of its customers, a financial organization must be not only good at storing sensitive data but making them available for the users whenever they require it. You can enhance such services by migrating to the cloud. In fact, the trend towards the cloud is already underway. <u>72% of US finance executives say</u>[11] they are either using cloud-based solutions or plan to do so in the future. Simultaneously, for new applications and services, nearly 40% of companies are adopting a cloud-first strategy. Cloud migration of a substantial financial organization will face some challenges like security issues, potential risks, cost, and strategy. Care should be taken by developing a strategy, deciding on the type of cloud, migration service provider, migration tools, hiring professionals, and later maintaining it. This provides you with an extensive overview of how you can approach the migration for optimal results.

Overview of Artificial Intelligence-Based Cloud Planning and Migration to Cut the Cost of Cloud.

Cloud Migration and planning transforms from the original Information Technology platform the user's services, data, and application hosted on in-house or cloud environment servers, to 1 or more cloud setting, intending to reduce the IT management and cloud cost while improving the performance of the Information Technology system. Artificial Intelligence planning and Automated planning have been examined expansively by analysts and effectively function in many areas for periods, such as in the health care industry, semiconductor manufacturing, and aviation industry (Hongtan Sun, Maja Vukovic, John Rofrano, Chen Lin). However, as the enterprises and IT applications and infrastructure started their journey towards digital transformation, they may have forced them to go over the initially allocated budget or may face several unexpected challenges.

In various situations, cloud planning and migration processes are not augmented to the or from the very beginning they were inadequately planned. So, how to allocate the optimal resources desirable for cloud planning and migration? In this, we will realize the most profitable advantages of getting into the cloud using Artificial Intelligence techniques and will go through the cloud migration budgeting and planning essentials. Without any interference, the cloud migrating applications are revised at the backend, therefore resulting in enhanced functionality and improved organization-wide stability.

At the same time, more and more enterprises and IT applications and infrastructure are considering their way and moving to Hybrid Cloud or Cloud service platforms. In their way, Artificial Intelligence promises Cloud planning and Migration flexibility, scalability, security, high performance, cost-effectiveness, and hypothetically lowering the cost of the resources, which is in general called the Cloud Migration (Hongtan Sun, Maja Vukovic, John Rofrano, Chen Lin). Planning and Migrating towards the cloud infrastructure, the enterprises will have to capitalize a convinced lump sum amount to move their operational setting in the cloud and plan for the cloud capacity in use and the regular ongoing expenditures. For some enterprises and IT applications and infrastructure organizations, planning and migrating to the cloud can enable them to enhance the overall user experience for their customers and thus will improve performance reducing latency.

When your company is planning its migration towards Cloud, the company will start by defining the operational settings that are involved in the migration. Their starting point can be a private hosting environment, an on-premises environment, or another public cloud environment. According to experts, Artificial Intelligence, and the cloud blend perfectly in a variety of ways, and Artificial Intelligence might just be the advanced technology to revolutionize Cloud planning and Migration solutions. AI as a service improves engenders new paths to the development of different solutions while cutting the cost of the cloud.

Analysis:

Cloud planning and Migration is not a cheap process:

Cloud planning and Migration is not a cheap, quick, or informal process. But the problems of not moving towards beneficial solutions such as rebuilding the legacy systems or applications for the cloud means competitive, technological, and debt drawbacks in agility and the exasperated users will be left experiencing poor user experiences. Enterprises and IT applications and infrastructure industries need to decide which system application to keep on and which to be moved to the cloud and premise. Then, these organizations must decide how to create a hybrid-cloud setup or refactor those system applications with cloudnative technologies, but it is a complicated process.

How the new data-driven system delivers insights into workflows:

The services like Synapse are used to calculate analyze and collect current and actionable data of cloud analytics that can impact business operations and delivers insights into workflows and processes (Diamandakis, 2020). The new data-driven system applications are starting life and moving or running in the cloud. The conventional enterprises such as Capital One as well as the innate online corporate such as Netflix have almost no physical data center and multibillion-dollar appraisals by implementing t Artificial Intelligence-based Cloud planning and Migration to cut the cost of the cloud, and they are not the only ones (AI and the cloud: Reduce risks, run smarter, 2019).

Cost comparison of cloud migration based on official API or 3rd party API.

Each decent strategy of cloud migration and planning makes efficient use of tools automated and designed to modernize the data transfer of your organization. Google Cloud, Azure,

Amazon Web Services, and many third-party software vendors have shaped data migration and planning tools for these purposes. You will need to think about the functionality, price, and compatibility while selecting which of these tools is best suited for your business organization (Cloud Migration Tools: Transferring Your Data with Ease, 2019). Cloud-based planning and migration storage tools have several compensations, such as low scalability, minimal fixed costs, and per-GB prices; however, while these solutions involve practical cost analysis of cloud storage and usage-based pricing plans (Niklas Krumm, Noah Hoffman, 2020).

3rd party Application Programming Interfaces provides 1 million free invocations per month and are universal to public cloud breadwinners. But you could end up with a substantial amount if you use 5 million invocations each month. An initiative that uses the wait-and-see method could go upwards of $100,000 per month and = end up with cloud bills. Cloud based planning and migration storage tools can make endorsements for better cost efficiency, such as use Application Programming Interfaces during peak-off hours a time to purchase API calls ahead of demand, and to take advantage of significantly reduced prices when the cloud provider proposes a discount (Linthicum, 2017).

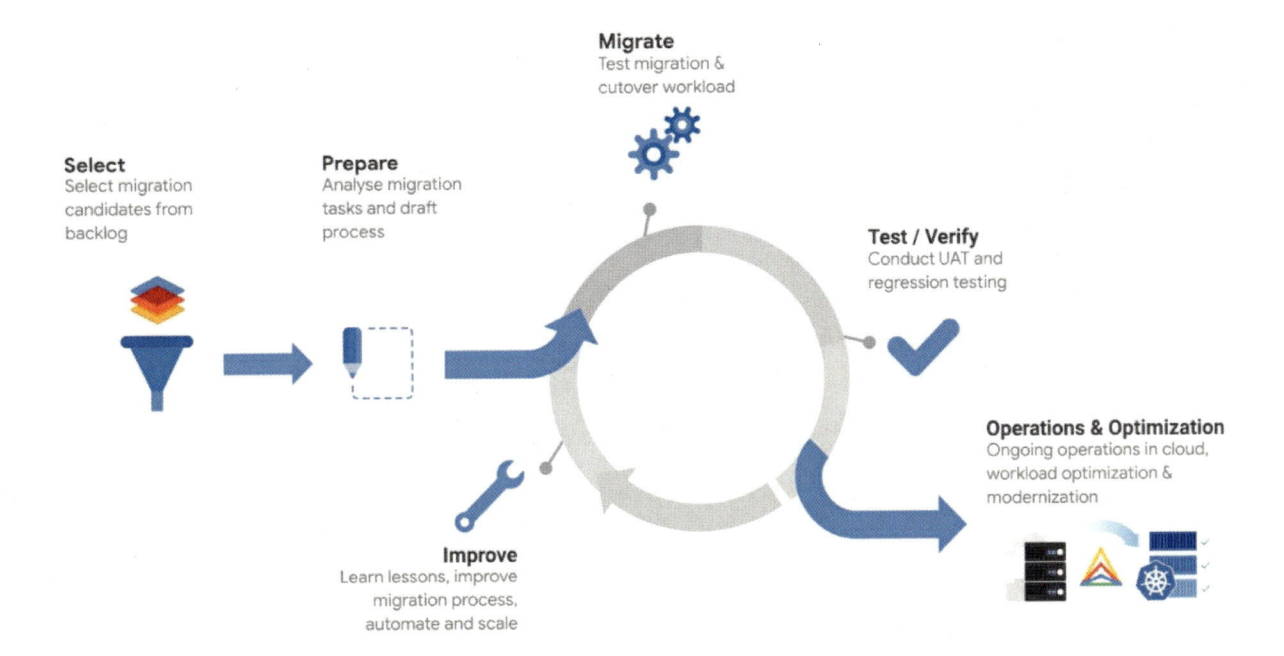

System Diagram: Important considerations for building a cloud migration:

https://cloud.google.com/blog/products/cloud-migration/planning-for-a-successful-cloudmigration Findings:

Deploying and building machine-learning and artificial intelligence models and techniques in planning and migrating towards the cloud is not computationally, but the cost is often cheap when the finer points of the enterprise's data infrastructure use the AI services that processes, stores, extract, egress, and ingress data (Gossett, 2020).

The data operations platform uses AI-powered cloud migration Recommendations:

The only data operations platform Unravel Data provides AI-powered recommendations and full-stack visibility in modern data applications to operate more scalable and reliable in performance. Unravel Data has proclaimed a new cloud planning and migration evaluation to help enterprises and IT applications and infrastructure organizations to move their workloads and data to Google Cloud, Azure, Amazon Web Services faster and with reduced cost. Unravel Data has built an adaptive and goal-driven solution with a reduced cost that will exclusively provide inclusive particulars of the system applications and source environment operating on it. The platform will determine the optimal cloud topology and identifies workloads and data suitable for the cloud-based on the anticipated hourly costs and business strategy. The platform also provides other critical insights to improve application performance, actionable recommendations, and as well as enables cloud capacity planning and chargeback reporting (Desk, 2019).

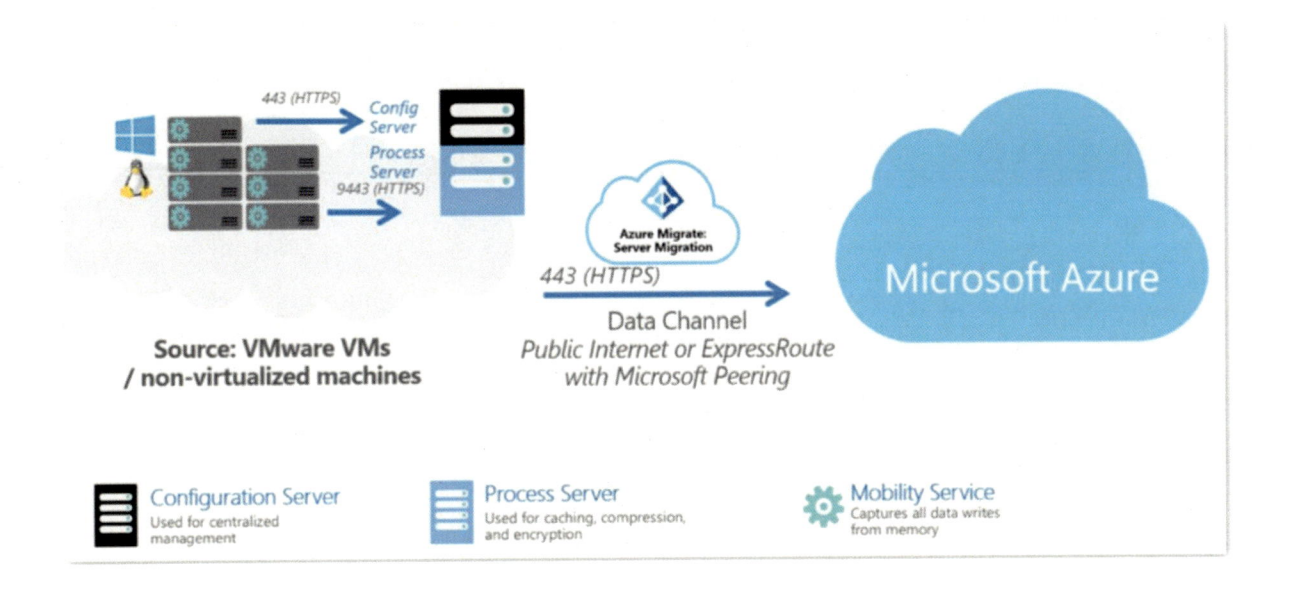

Diagram: 1 Azure Server Migration Service

https://cloud.netapp.com/blog/cloud-migrationtools-transferring-your-data-with-ease

Unfortunately, enterprises and IT applications, and infrastructure organizations that plan and migrate the cloud manually are not capable to fulfil the expectations as the process of migrating to the cloud takes longer and becomes more difficult than anticipated. In this way, it would be difficult to optimize costs and it will rise higher than forecasted apps (Desk, 2019).

The journey to align the business outcomes and migrating towards the cloud is technically a complex process and sometimes be challenging. But the Artificial Intelligence-based

Cloud planning and Migration software will help the organizations to takes the error-prone and guesswork manual practices out of the box to provide a variety of critical data insights and thus cut the cost of the cloud.

The AI-driven assessment will enable enterprises and IT applications and infrastructure organizations to:

Discover detailed usage and current clusters to make an informed and effective plan and move to the cloud.

Prioritize and identify certain system application data workloads such as decoupled storage and elastic scaling to advantage from cloud native.

Capabilities:

Cloud migrating platforms are part of the larger platforms such as (SaaS) Software-as-a Service, to deliver more value to their customers.

Define the optimal cloud topology that minimizes risks or costs and matches a certain business strategy and goals.

On the amount of storage space required, the users of the system get specific instance types of artificial intelligence recommendations with the option to choose between object storage and local attached.

When moving and planning to the cloud and obtaining the incur hourly costs expected, it will allow the system users to contrast and compare different cloud services and providers costs and for different goals.

Across Infrastructure as a Service and Managed Hadoop or Spark Platform as a service, it will be beneficial to compare the costs for different cloud options.

Users may have received volume discounts that have been incorporated in the default OnDemand cloud prices.

Benefits of migrating to the cloud:

Scalability and Greater Flexibility. Despite on-premises infrastructure, Cloud computing can scale up to greater numbers of users far more easily and support larger workloads and data, which requires enterprises and IT applications and infrastructure organizations to set up and purchase additional networking equipment, physical servers, or software licenses. The teams working remotely will deploy, fix issues, or update various machines being used. The procedure will make it a more flexible and scalable solution.

Cost Reduction:

The Artificial Intelligence-based Cloud planning and Migration software will help the cloud providers handle maintenance and upgrades that take the error-prone and guesswork manual practices out of the box to provide a variety of critical data insights and thus cut the cost of the cloud. In this way, they can reduce the cost they spend on IT or other operations. The AI-driven assessment will enable enterprises and IT applications and infrastructure organizations to discover detailed usage and current clusters to make an informed and effective plan and move to the cloud.

Performance:

For some enterprises and IT applications and infrastructure organizations, planning and migrating to the cloud can enable them to enhance the overall user experience for their customers and thus will improve performance reducing latency.

Reduced Infrastructure Complexity

Cloud systems reduce the infrastructure complexity that motivates the structural design being used to make them all work together and provides new machines to the needed services.

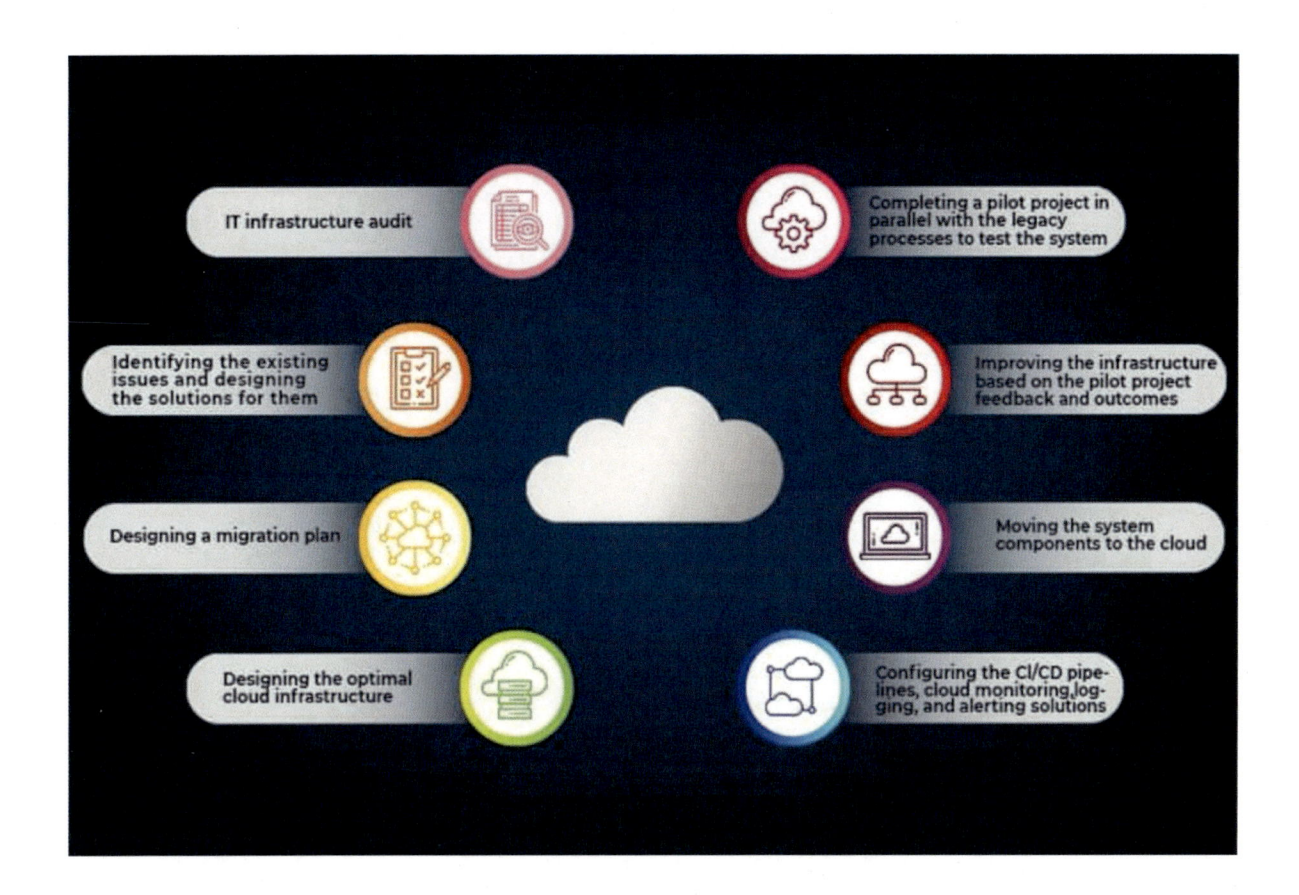

Diagram 3: Benefits of moving towards cloud migration
https://images.app.goo.gl/X57YQHChU3PwC45N9

Advantages of Artificial Intelligence-based Cloud planning and Migration

Here are enlisted various advantages of Artificial Intelligence-based Cloud planning and

Migration:

Artificial intelligence powers cloud planning and Migration that acts as an engine to increase the impact and scope Artificial Intelligence has in the greater market.

IT infrastructure organizations use Artificial intelligence-based cloud planning and Migration tools to help automate repetitive tasks and streamline workloads (Hongtan Sun, Maja Vukovic, John Rofrano, Chen Lin).

IT infrastructure organizations are moving towards improving data management processes. Artificial Intelligence-based Cloud planning and Migration tools can help modernize the way data is updated, ingested, and accomplished, so economic organizations easily submit precise real-time data to clients.

Optimal cloud topology using Machine Learning algorithms minimizes risks or costs and matches a certain business strategy and goals.

AI-powered recommendations and full-stack visibility are provided by cloud migrating platforms in modern data applications to operate more scalable and reliable in performance.

As mostly cloud migrating platforms are part of the larger platforms such as (SaaS) Software-as-a-Service, to deliver more value to their customers.

Optimal cloud migrating solutions offer greater value to the end-users and provide enhanced functionality.

Without any interference, the cloud migrating applications are revised at the backend, therefore resulting in enhanced functionality and improved organization-wide stability. Cloud migrating solutions for enterprises and IT infrastructure organizations provide a major advantage i.e., mobility to access important applications that it offers for all the employees working in the organizations (Cloud Migration Tools: Transferring Your Data with Ease, 2019).

It has a reduced cost feature that can spontaneously alter the rating on a given outcome to account for issues such as inventory levels, demand, market trends, and competitor sales.

Disadvantages of Artificial Intelligence-based Cloud planning and Migration

Here are enlisted a few disadvantages of Artificial Intelligence-based Cloud planning and Migration:

As the data has been migrated and shared to the cloud in its wholeness, so it might be possible that the data may get lost and might eventually leak out.

The cloud migration process is a time-intensive process that requires cautious data evaluation and planning, if not taken care of properly, your precious data might be lost, and in certain cases, irretrievable.

When data is planned and migrated from the existing systems to the cloud, specific protection needs to be carried, and all the data security variables need to be patterned off. There are certain interoperability issues while transferring data to the cloud, which means that each software vendor considers cloud migration in their understandings, therefore the process will be tough for specific system applications to connect with each other (CLOUD MIGRATION - ADVANTAGES, DISADVANTAGES, AND HOW TO MITIGATE RISKS, 2019). When implementing a cloud migration strategy for an enterprise-wide system, it is necessary to recollect the time that the procedure will take, because it will sometimes take more time than required.

Conclusion

The paper helps you design, plan, and execute the method of migrating your data and workloads to the Cloud. Now many enterprises and IT applications and infrastructure organizations are moving towards planning and migrating Hybrid Cloud or Cloud service platforms. In their way, Artificial Intelligence promises Cloud planning and Migration flexibility, scalability, security, high performance, cost-effectiveness, and hypothetically lowering the cost of the resources, minimizes risks, mobility to access important applications, and matches a certain business strategy and goals. The paper highlights the major platform Unravel Data, which provides a critical insight to improve application performance, actionable recommendations, and as well as enables cloud capacity planning and chargeback reporting. The cloud-enabled software help organizations to enhance the overall user experience for their customers and thus will improve performance reducing latency. It will be beneficial to compare the costs for different cloud options. Meanwhile, if data has not cared properly, it may get lost and might eventually leak out. So, it is a time-intensive process that requires cautious data evaluation and planning.

References:

https://technative.io/ai-and-the-cloud-reduce-risks-run-smarter/

CLOUD MIGRATION - ADVANTAGES, DISADVANTAGES, AND HOW TO MITIGATE RISKS.

(2019).

Retrieved from flatworld: https://www.flatworldsolutions.com/ITservices/articles/cloud-migration-advantages-disadvantages-risk-mitigation.php Cloud Migration Tools: Transferring Your Data with Ease.

Retrieved from netapp: https://cloud.netapp.com/blog/cloud-migration-tools-transferring-your-data-withease

Desk, A. N. (2019, 8 1). Unravel Introduces Cloud Migration Assessment Offer to Reduce Costs and Accelerate the Transition of Data Workloads to Azure, AWS or Google Cloud. Retrieved from aithority: https://aithority.com/computing/unravel-introduces-cloudmigration-assessment-offer-to-reduce-costs-and-accelerate-the-transition-of-dataworkloads-to-azure-aws-or-google-cloud/

Diamandakis, V. (2020). Putting AI and Machine Learning to Work in Cloud-Based BI and Analytics.

Gossett, S. (2020, 3 17). HOW TO REDUCE AI COMPUTING COSTS. Retrieved from builtin: https://builtin.com/artificial-intelligence/ai-computing-cost-reduction

Hongtan Sun, Maja Vukovic, John Rofrano, Chen Lin. (n.d.). Advantages and Challenges of Using AI Planning in Cloud Migration. 2.

Linthicum, D. (2017, 8 7). API prices create cloud billing shock for some enterprises. Retrieved from search cloud computing: https://searchcloudcomputing.techtarget.com/tip/API-prices-create-cloud-billing-shock-forsome-enterprises

Niklas Krumm, Noah Hoffman. (2020). Practical estimation of cloud storage costs for clinical genomic data. Practical Laboratory Medicine.

------------------------------end_of-the_document------------------

Made in the USA
Middletown, DE
10 February 2025